06/10
3⁰⁰

14-

D0532250

Cooking Class

♦ ♦ ♦

A chef's step-by-step guide to stress-free
dinner parties that are simply elegant!

Carol Dearth, CCP

Here's to great dinners with wonderful friends!

Carol Dearth

Copyright © 2003 by Carol Dearth

ISBN: 0-9740825-0-3

For additional copies or information contact:
Fork in the Road Publishers
1883 145th Place Southeast
Bellevue, Washington 98007
(425) 644-4285
or
raincitycookingschool.com

Design: David Marty Design
Photography: Randolph S. Dearth
Food Styling: Carol Dearth

All rights reserved. No part of this book may be reproduced
or transmitted in any form by any means, electronic or mechanical,
including photocopying and recording, or by any information
storage or retrieval system, except as may be expressly permitted
by the 1976 Copyright Act or in writing by the publisher.

Printed in Korea

Dedicated to Randy,
Because you have always been my biggest fan,
both in the kitchen and out.

Acknowledgements

I would like to thank my family and all of those friends for helping and cheering this book on, and for making this book possible.

First and foremost, my family: Randy, Ryan and Jim Dearth; who were patient, and who wore many hats during the production of this book. Their support and insight is invaluable. And a special mention for my late father-in-law, Jim Dearth, whose vision was unbounding.

And to all of my friends, for pestering and questioning me, for pointing me in the right direction, for the testing, reading and re-reading, and for reminding me that it was time to get on with things. For that I have many thanks to Tiki Mitchell, Amy Britt, Jay Chase, Susan Burkhard, Dottie Stickley, Darlene Warnken, Ann Parrish, Margi Smith, Beth Munns, Larry Munns, Susannah Stuart, Judy Witts, CCP, Chef John Power, and Gwen Walters, CCP. I am truly blessed to have such wonderful people in my life.

The chicken was rubbery, complimented by the oh-so-sticky rice. And the chocolate mousse was, well, "chalklike." No, actually it was inedible. My first dinner party. I was nervous, embarrassed and disappointed at the result. My guests were gracious, but still hungry. Now nearly 27 years later, I am continually queried for the secrets to entertaining successfully and easily. My entertaining skills have been carefully honed and augmented by my experiences. For 26 of those 27 years, I have been a Navy wife, with the opportunities to travel, live, enjoy and study cooking around the world. I have also had the opportunity to entertain in my own home, from dinner for four to cocktails for more than 200! Like learning to play an instrument I have developed my skills in practice, guided by instruction. I've been taught by masters in the culinary field and learned a lot of tricks along the way.

In the early 80's the Navy moved my family to Naples, Italy, where we immediately fell in love with the food. I spent those two years studying informally, mastering our favorites. I traveled around the Mediterranean collecting recipes and sampling the food. We call that "research." Friends hounded me to teach them the unique cuisines. My college degree is in Health Education, adult education techniques with background in nutrition, biology and chemistry. And so the metamorphosis to cooking teacher began to occur.

Teaching always raises more questions, and the search for answers led me to cuisine school. In 1994 while living in Northern Virginia, I started cuisine training at a satellite school of Peter Kump's New York Cooking School. Of course, we moved yet again, so my formal cuisine studies began in the east and finished on the West Coast two years later at a small school near my current home. Alas, we left the Northwest once again, this time for San Diego. But there were more cardboard boxes in store for me. Three years after arriving in San Diego we were offered orders to London. I listened — opportunity was knocking. What a great location. Our flat was a mere six blocks from Le Cordon Bleu, London. I seized the chance to study pastry and cooking theory, finishing off with a Master Chef Catering course.

My time in Italy and around the Mediterranean taught me about fresh, seasonal simple food. In Virginia I learned about classic American cuisine. In the northwest the specialties are seafood and Asian fusion. In San Diego I learned about fresh ingredients, dining al fresco, and the cuisine of Baja. London presented the opportunity to travel about Europe once again and "research" Continental cuisine. Now as a chef, I can choose from the myriad of cuisines to which I have been exposed in my travels and studies, and my teaching and learning experiences around the globe.

Teaching about food is unique; few other subjects involve all five senses. We see the beautiful colors of a well-presented plate. The aroma entices and intrigues, possibly triggering memories of another time. Food sizzles, hisses, crackles and snaps. We must handle the food to prepare it — chopping, kneading, rolling, pounding and stirring can be very therapeutic. Touching food with our hands, lips and tongues we check: is it hot? cold? done? And finally we taste, savoring our creation. A well-prepared meal is truly a sensual experience, which explains why we feel so satisfied after a wonderful repast. I have a passion to teach cooking!

We are all a sum of our experiences. My food is somewhat eclectic, a bit of sophisticated but uncomplicated French, the intense fresh simple flavors of Italian, a dash of Mediterranean, the purity of the Northwest and the festivity of Mexican. It is not fusion food. The true character of the dish remains intact, with simple steps and great technique. I like to enhance the natural flavors of the food, not mask them. Over the years I have tested, tweaked and refined my recipes to produce the best possible food simply and successfully. I use recipes in cooking classes as vehicles to teach techniques. I believe that mastering a cooking technique requires a basic knowledge of the theory and science behind the technique. Science and explanations of cooking theory are an integral part of my classes, and now this book. Once a technique is mastered it can be applied to other recipes. Like the adage of "Give a man a fish and feed him for a day, teach a man to fish and feed him for a lifetime (or get rid of him on weekends)." My goal for my students and for you as my reader is for you to become more confident cooks. If you understand what is happening in the pot, you are more likely to produce a successful result.

Great dishes originate from good quality ingredients. I emphasize the knowledge of ingredients, how and where to purchase and store, along with food safety concerns. Having the right tool for the job makes cooking easier and more fun. At my school I discuss the tools of the trade in class, and you will find special information on "The Right Tool" in the book. And there are the tricks of the trade from a chef's point of view. Then the test: we must eat what we have prepared! But first, we eat with our eyes, so we properly present and garnish the dish. A final toast to the chefs and we wash it down with the appropriate wine. Another fine meal gone to waist.

Over the years I have not only sought information, but also shared and taught cooking techniques as well as catering tips and food theory to my students around the country and the globe. Each of my clients comes to me with his or her own special needs and agenda, but the recurring theme of questions always revolves around how to organize and prepare a special meal for guests. A large number of my students are insecure or overwhelmed with entertaining guests, feeling that they need better cooking skills, or that entertaining is risky business. Using my many years of experience providing hands-on cooking instruction augmented by my broad-based professional culinary education, I hope to provide you with professional tools and techniques with which you can plan, organize, prepare and present elegant dinner parties at home. You will become a better cook, making more successful meals and more stress-free parties. The techniques and guides in Cooking Class are applicable and transferable to all cooking situations. So relax and enjoy.

Last year my studying and experience paid big dividends: I joined an elite group earning my Certified Culinary Professionals (CCP), a designation from the International Association of Culinary Professionals. Having vowed never to move again, I am now the proprietor of RainCity Cooking School in Bellevue, Washington.

Contents

Introduction

Introduction

My goals in writing this book are to inspire you to have friends and acquaintances over for dinner; to be successful at entertaining; to enjoy the experience; and to join in the fun yourself.

In my many years of teaching cooking around the country and the globe, I have been repeatedly surprised at how many people today are insecure with entertaining guests. Many feel that they need better cooking skills, or that entertaining is risky business. Or that the task is just too much to fit into their busy schedules, with guest lists, menus, cooking, setting up, and all.

This book aims to bridge that gap, to show you how easy it can be to organize, prepare and present a fabulous meal, while enjoying the experience. I have included a Master Dinner Party Plan in this section to streamline the party planning and preparation for any menu you choose. Each menu has a customized Cook's Master Plan. This Cook's plan details when to prepare all of the items in your menu on a timeline. Designed for ease of preparation, each recipe includes information on making it ahead, and how to put the dish "on hold" so that you can easily make a similar plan for other dinners. To improve your cooking skills and understanding of the process you will find tips and techniques, as well as information on ingredients and tools.

The recipes in this book are arranged according to seasonal menus, but they are meant only as guides. You may want to mix and match your own favorite recipes and create your own menus. If there is an item you don't like on the menu, just browse through the book for a substitution. The recipes are nearly all designed to serve four. They are all easily doubled or tripled as your guest list expands. Or divide them in half for an intimate dinner for two.

You may choose to use these recipes or others, or use purchased prepared foods as still another option. But having fun is not an option — it is a requirement! So relax, and know that you can do it with ease and style, all the while enjoying the process.

Planning

A wise person once said "Failure to plan is planning to fail." Use these tools to make your party easy to organize, prepare and present a beautiful meal for your guests.

Planning

HOW TO HAVE A SUCCESSFUL DINNER PARTY

MASTER DINNER PARTY PLAN

How to Have a Successful Dinner Party

We invite friends into our homes to break bread, to have an opportunity to spend time with the people we enjoy and to show them that they are special to us. Always remember that the main idea is to be with your guests.

Entertaining is a process. The best way to learn is to start small, have a dinner party, and enjoy your success! It doesn't have to be as scary as it sounds!

If you are hosting your first dinner party, start by inviting a few close friends over for an informal meal. This would be a good time to try one of the simpler menus in the book. A party of four is a good start. If this is not your first effort at entertaining, I hope that this book will help to add class and style to your efforts, and increase your confidence. Regardless, the most important rule of thumb, no matter how many times you entertain, is MAKE IT SIMPLE! Being organized and streamlining your preparation will make things easier for you both before and during your party. Remember that people come to socialize, to talk to one another, and to meet new friends. Your guests will feel more comfortable, and things will flow more smoothly when you are relaxed and enjoying yourself. Making things simple will allow you to host a classy event and spend more time with your guests.

The main elements for a successful party generate from your thoughtfulness and planning: the guests, the setting, the atmosphere and the meal. With a little practice you can combine them artistically every time with confidence. A very wise person once told me "Failing to plan is planning to fail." The Master Dinner Party Plan included in this section will be invaluable in your planning. Use it as a checklist to insure success.

First, decide your guest list.

How many people should you invite? A small, intimate gathering of close friends is by far the easiest and a good start if you are a novice. But small gatherings of people who don't know each other well can prove more challenging. A party of four is very simple, compared to a party of eight or more. If you are just beginning to learn about entertaining, keep the numbers small. If and when you are ready to expand your horizons, add a few more acquaintances. For larger gatherings, try to invite a good mixture of your friends, a few new people, a group having diverse occupations, hobbies and interests. It is always more interesting to meet someone new than to rehash old topics. Careful thought into the *people ingredients* of the evening is perhaps more crucial than the food ingredients of your meal. The end result of this mixture should be FUN!

Next, set a date.

In these busy times, it is important to invite guests well in advance. For an informal dinner, invitations should be extended at least a week ahead. More formal occasions, or parties for which you are inviting people you don't know as well, require the courtesy of at least two weeks' notice. For larger events, allow at least a month. Consider requesting an RSVP for planning purposes. Invitations can be extended by telephone, or written, depending on the circumstances. Keep in mind, that you may not be able to reach the people you wish to invite right away by telephone until it is too close to the scheduled date and they have made other plans. If you are inviting by telephone, do remember to give your guests a definite time, so that neither you nor they are unexpectedly surprised or inconvenienced.

If you have quite a number of people to entertain, you may want to divide the list and consider hosting two events, one night after the other. Sound like a colossal effort? Maybe, but in reality you will save time and money, as you can use the same centerpiece, and serve the same menu. If you choose an appetizer and dessert that can be made well ahead of time for both meals, the second evening becomes SO EASY! And, as you clean up from the first party, you can set up for the second one. This idea has worked very well for me.

Make your guests feel special.

Ambiance is another word for atmosphere. Reflect on your own personal experiences when you have had the pleasure of being a guest. It is important to create a warm, comfortable feeling when entertaining. Whether you invite one or eighty, make your guests feel welcome in your home, and in your presence. Isn't it wonderful to feel special and pampered? But that is just part of the ambiance. You can add to the warm and inviting mood of your home with music, a fire, candles, and flowers. When you want to pull out all the stops, you might want to consider napkin folds, menus or place cards. Experiment with a variety of these little "extras," one addition at a time, so that each item is manageable and you can see how much time each requires as well as how each contributes to the whole.

Being organized means that you are in control of your time, not rushed. Allow enough time before serving the main meal to visit with guests, possibly enjoy a cocktail or an hors d'oeurve. Half an hour is about right. Bear in mind that hors d'oeurves are supposed to stimulate the appetite, not satisfy it. A little food is just enough. Set the pace so that your guests don't feel rushed into dinner or through the meal.

Now for a menu.

If you are a novice, I suggest you use one of the menus already prepared. As your confidence builds, or if you are an experienced host or hostess you can substitute or mix and match dishes, bearing in mind that you will need to reorganize your Master Plan to accommodate the changes. Your menu may be influenced by the style of party, whether a formal or informal dinner, a buffet, or an outdoor dinner. Try to MAKE IT SIMPLE, keeping in mind items that can be prepared in advance, maybe even frozen, and simply thawed and reheated the day of the party. Consider which seasonal ingredients will be available. You may choose to augment your menu with a few purchased prepared items to save time.

If you decide to plan your own menu, start with the main dish first; then choose the side dishes to accompany it. The appetizer and dessert can be selected next. Try to balance these: if one is heavy, the other should be lighter. What else do you need to round out the menu? Maybe an hors d'oeurve, a salad, bread, flavored butters, garnishes, wines, other beverages and after dinner drinks. Write it all down, in logical order. Then go back and look at your menu as a whole. Look for balance and harmony, foods that compliment one another in flavor, color and texture. Keeping portions small, your guests will still have room for dessert, even after three or four previous courses.

It's always a good idea to plan a menu around foods you know you prepare well. If you are trying a new recipe, you may want to try a "dry run" on your family before serving it to guests. This will give you a chance for a preparation rehearsal, as well as an opportunity to taste and maybe add your own personal touches to the recipes. It will also give you the opportunity to customize your preparation timeline and presentation ideas.

As you plan, consider the amount of time required to make each dish. Usually one or two complicated foods are plenty, and they will showcase better if accompanied by simpler foods. This is a big part of MAKING IT SIMPLE; complex recipes are much more manageable if you can do them ahead. Also consider the available equipment — is your refrigerator large enough to store large platters? Do you have a large enough roasting pan, etc.? Will all of the cooking be one the stovetop or in the oven (will it all fit)? And don't forget food safety considerations. Keep food out of that 'danger zone' from 40°F to 140°F. Serve hot foods hot and cold foods cold.

More planning.

How will you serve the food? Your method of service will dictate the amount of food to prepare as well as set-up plans. Plan on one portion of each dish per guest for sit-down service, half again as much for buffet style for the entree and accompanying side dishes. For dessert, again, one portion per guest for sit-down service, two portions for buffet. If your crowd is larger than 12 people, allow 2 to 3 portions of both entree and dessert per guest. You don't want to run out of food before you run out of guests!

I recommend serving the main course and dessert at the table for your party of four. You may choose to have the appetizer more buffet style, in the living room before you seat your guests. Service at the table is more elegant and formal. Decide if you will serve "family style" or if you prefer to set up each plate in the kitchen. But for a crowd of eight or more, a buffet may be easier.

Check the special section on buffets for more tips. If you choose buffet style, will your guests be seated at a table after serving themselves, or will they be sitting with food in their laps. Do be sure that each guest will have a place to sit. Will you need trays? You may choose to have the main meal served as a buffet, but dessert presented on individual plates at the table. Or serve the appetizer buffet-style, dinner may be served with your guests seated at the table, and a simple dessert in the living room. A combination of styles can create an element of surprise, especially if you have created a show-stopping dessert!

Will you need help? Older children can be encouraged to help with entertaining, as well as sons or daughters of friends. They feel important, and included in the party, while getting valuable training and experience. You may need help with early or last minute preparations, setting up, answering the door, taking coats, or serving food and drinks. I have used this avenue many times with great success. Don't forget to reward your hard working 'staff' at the end of the night. Praise and money are always gratefully accepted. You may want them to work for you again!

By following the Master Dinner Party Plan and the Cook's Master Plan you can break the preparations down into small, more easily accomplished tasks. Don't stress out. You will have a beautiful party.

Master Dinner Party Plan

The secret to giving successful parties is confidence coupled with organization, both of which come from experience. Here are some tips to make any party look low-maintenance, and to make it feel that way, too! Your guests will wonder how you managed to pull off such an elegant dinner party so effortlessly.

Much of the preparation for any meal can be done in advance of the dinner party, leaving you more time to relax and enjoy your guests. Following a master plan will reduce the anxiety factor, making for a painless experience. I have included a master work plan for each of the sixteen dinner party menus in this book. You may want to develop and save your own work plan for a particularly successful party, utilizing it in varied forms in the future.

As far ahead as possible:

Set your guest list and menu. If necessary, make two lists: one for guests, which can later be used for RSVP response; and one for the menu.

The menu can then become your master plan for preparation.

- Lists where each of the recipes is found (book and page number for example).

- How many of each recipe will you need? (Nearly all of the recipes in this book are designed to serve four.)

- How early can each recipe be prepared? If any of the items chosen can be prepared weeks in advance and frozen, DO IT! You'll be less stressed later and have more time the day of the party.

- Which serving pieces will be used for each recipe? Pick out platters, plates or bowls and serving utensils for each recipe including trivets, etc.

Several days ahead:

Check your menu, including the wines and non-alcoholic drinks. Read through each recipe you still need to prepare and highlight all of the ingredients that you need to buy. Check how many each recipe will serve. Make two shopping lists: one for only the freshest ingredients to purchase the day before the party; and one for everything else to be purchased right away. Don't forget condiments, paper supplies, and ice.

Pick out the music you want to play and set up the music equipment.

Decide what you are going to wear; the last thing you want is to discover something needs to be dry-cleaned or pressed as your guests are ringing the doorbell.

Press any linens and fold the napkins, if desired.

Three days ahead:

Chop and measure foods, such as nuts or chopped vegetables for sauces or casseroles that may be refrigerated in plastic bags.

Two days ahead:

Prepare the foods that may be refrigerated, and store in covered dishes: molded salads, salad dressings, sauces, desserts. Chop and slice salad ingredients; refrigerate in plastic bags.

The day before:

Shop for fresh ingredients on your list. Wash and dry all produce, wrap salad greens in paper towels, and put in plastic bags and refrigerate. Prepare fruit for salads or desserts. Cover with plastic wrap and refrigerate.

Thaw items that were previously frozen, and put into serving dishes if possible. Prepare casseroles, vegetables, desserts or any dishes that can be refrigerated overnight.

Prepare any garnishes that can be made ahead.

Chill the wines and other cold beverages. Make ice.

Clean the guest powder room and make sure it is stocked with sufficient hand towels, soap and other supplies.

Designate an area for hanging coats; if the weather is inclement, you don't want wet garments thrown on your bed.

Set the table, arrange the flowers, and candles, if desired. Put any non-food items and serving pieces out (salt and pepper, wine coasters, etc.). Put extras such as butter on serving plates or in dishes; wrap and refrigerate. Set up a tray for after-dinner coffee/tea. On the day of the party, you will have saved yourself a large chunk of time.

If you are having cocktails and hors d'oeurves in an area other than the dining table, set up for that as well, with glasses and napkins, bowls of nuts or other cocktail snacks.

Plan tasks for those who invariably ask "What can I do to help?" Hand them an apron and put them to work with the last minute preparations such as filling water glasses, lighting candles, opening wine, plating salads. This way, you can visit with your guests and enjoy a cocktail while you finish preparing the meal.

The morning of the party:

Remove all food that has not been thawed from the freezer and thaw as directed. Place foods to be cooked in appropriate cooking dishes; refrigerate or place near the stove.

Garnish desserts. Assemble salads. Unmold and garnish molded salads.

Set up for coffee/tea, cream and sugar for after dinner.

Take a deep breath, you're doing fine!

Before your guests arrive:

Cook and heat foods as necessary. Arrange any foods on the table if appropriate.

Warm the dinner plates or serving dishes. This is an especially nice touch, and helps to keep the food hot as you are plating it. The easiest way to do this is to put plates in the oven, heat it to 160°F. This is also a good place to hold hot foods until you are ready to serve them. If your oven is not available, you can warm plates in the dry cycle of your dishwasher, or cover them with very hot water in the sink.

When your guests arrive, greet them with a smile, relax and enjoy their company. Your guests will enjoy the occasion if you're having a good time too.

Whatever happens, don't point out when things go wrong and DON'T PANIC! Far more likely than not, a recipe you accidentally overcooked will not be noticed by your guests as long as you don't announce the mistake. Remember that a great party has a life of its own, independent of your plans. Relax and enjoy it yourself, and your guests will too. Relax…breathe…it's a beautiful party.

Summer

A time to relax, put your feet up, enjoy
the long, warm, lazy days of the season,
along with the bounty of fresh fruits and
vegetables from the market, or your own
garden. Put a relaxed atmosphere on your
dinner party as well, by being organized
well in advance. Make the best use of
Mother Nature by presenting more fresh
fruits and vegetables in their natural state,
saving you time. Time to relax…

Sicilian Chicken
Sicilian Broccoli & Cauliflower Salad
Roasted Potato Salad

Chocolate Shortcakes

Lemon Linguini with Fresh Tomato Sauce
and Grilled Chicken

Pear Sorbet

Scallops with Pink Grapefruit Sauce

Peaches in Champagne

Marinated "London Broil"
Vegetables with Capers
Rosemary Potatoes

R.S.V.P. Fruit Plate

Summer Menus

AL FRESCO DINNER ON THE PATIO

Greek Salad

Sicilian Chicken

Sicilian Broccoli & Cauliflower Salad

Roasted Potato Salad

Chocolate Shortcakes with Fresh Berries

CASUAL SUMMER EVENING

Marinated Shrimp

"Fizzy" Lemonade

Lemon Linguini with Fresh Tomato Sauce and Grilled Chicken

Pear Sorbet

MOONLIGHT SUMMER SOLSTICE SUPPER

Figs & Goat Cheese

Scallops with Pink Grapefruit Sauce

Seasoned Rice

Zucchini Ribbons

Peaches in Champagne

SUMPTUOUS SUMMER FETE

Caramelized Almond Roasted Dates

Tomato Basil Soup

Marinated "London Broil"

Vegetables with Capers

Rosemary Potatoes

R.S.V.P. Fruit Plate

Al Fresco Dinner on the Patio*

Greek Salad

◆

Sicilian Chicken

Sicilian Broccoli & Cauliflower Salad
and
Roasted Potato Salad

Assorted Breads
(purchased)

Pinot Gris
Served very cold

◆

Chocolate Shortcakes
With
Fresh Berries

◆

Coffee or Tea

*This menu can be prepared ahead,
chilled, packed and served
as an elegant picnic!

Al Fresco Dinner on the Patio

Three days ahead:
Prepare **Chocolate Shortcakes**, wrap and freeze.
Fold the napkins if desired.

Two days ahead:
Shop for vegetables for **Greek Salad**, **Broccoli and Cauliflower Salad**, **Roasted Potato Salad**.
Cut and steam broccoli and cauliflower for **Broccoli and Cauliflower Salad**. Wrap and refrigerate.
Cut peppers for **Broccoli and Cauliflower Salad**. Pit olives if necessary. Wrap and refrigerate.
Prepare dressing for **Broccoli and Cauliflower Salad**, refrigerate separately.

The day before:
Shop for fruit and cream for **Chocolate Shortcakes**.
Put butter on its serving plate or bowl, cover and refrigerate.
Chill the wine and other cold beverages.
Set up coffee or tea tray, after dinner drinks, glasses, etc.
Make ice.
Set the table. Put out any non-food items (salt and pepper, wine coaster, etc.)
Arrange the flowers.

The morning before:
Wash and cut vegetables for **Greek Salad** except onion. If space allows, combine and refrigerate on serving plates.
Crumble Feta for **Greek Salad**, cover and refrigerate.
Prepare **Roasted Potato Salad**. Arrange in serving bowl. Cover and refrigerate.
Set up coffee maker.

6 hours before guests arrive:
Truss and prepare chicken for **Sicilian Chicken**. Begin roasting chicken.
Remove **Chocolate Shortcakes** from freezer to thaw. Prepare fruit for shortcakes.

1 – 2 hours before guests arrive:
Prepare garnish for **Sicilian Chicken**; arrange on serving platter.
Remove butter from refrigerator to soften.
Slice purchased bread, if serving.

Before your guests arrive:
Slice onion for **Greek Salad**, **Broccoli and Cauliflower Salad**.
Combine vegetables for **Greek Salad**; dress and season. Sprinkle with Feta. Place on the table.
Combine ingredients for **Broccoli and Cauliflower Salad**. Arrange in serving bowl.
Allow **Roasted Potato Salad** to come to room temperature.
Preheat a platter for the chicken.

After the guests arrive:
Remove **Sicilian Chicken** from oven; let stand.
Prepare pan sauce for **Sicilian Chicken**.
Carve chicken if desired, arrange on serving platter.
Plate **Chocolate Shortcakes**, garnish and serve.

TECHNIQUE

PITTING OLIVES

Wonderful olives are easy to find in the deli section of your supermarket. But, the drawback is the pits. Olives don't have to be the pits!

To remove the pits easily, press firmly on each olive with the bowl of a wooden spoon, inverted so that the olive doesn't shoot out, across the room! Usually, a small tear will appear in the side of each olive. Just pull the pit out. Tah Dah!! NO MORE PITS!

✓ CUTTING BELL PEPPERS LIKE A PRO

To make bell peppers easy to handle, first cut a slice from the top, removing the stem and creating a flat surface. Cut a slice from the bottom as well. Stand the pepper on either of the cut surfaces, and cut down the sides, creating flat sections of pepper. This should also remove the core. The resulting flat sections are much easier to handle and cut into strips or dice.

Greek Salad

Many years ago I had the opportunity to visit Greece in the spring, where I first discovered this salad in the outdoor cafes. Crisp and colorful, bursting with flavors and freshness, it was my daily lunch with a cold glass of crisp white wine and some crusty bread. I still love it on a hot summer day.

4 ripe tomatoes, cored and coarsely chopped
1 cucumber, peeled and seeded, if desired, cut in ½ inch chunks
1 medium red onion, sliced and separated into rings
½ of a green bell pepper, chopped very coarsely
1½ red bell pepper, chopped very coarsely
½ yellow bell pepper, chopped very coarsely
16 black olives, preferably Greek
16 green olives, preferably Greek
2 teaspoons dried oregano
salt and freshly ground pepper to taste
4 tablespoons red wine vinegar
4 tablespoons olive oil
6 – 8 ounces Feta cheese, crumbled

Combine tomatoes, cucumber, red onion rings, peppers and olives in salad bowl. Sprinkle with oregano, salt and pepper. Toss with vinegar. Drizzle olive oil over vegetables; sprinkle Feta over top. Serve at room temperature.

Serves 4.

Sicilian Chicken

In Sicily, lemons are plentiful and used widely in the regional cooking. Succulent and juicy, this easy chicken dish is always a big hit with family or with a crowd! And it makes great picnic fare when served cold.

1 (2 – 3 pound) roasting chicken
salt and pepper
1 large lemon, pricked around with fork
2 tablespoons butter

fresh parsley
lemon slices or wedges

Preheat the oven to 350°F. Clean chicken, pat dry with paper towels. Liberally salt and pepper cavity of chicken and place lemon inside cavity. Rub outside of chicken with butter. Truss chicken as shown at right. Sprinkle outside of chicken generously with salt and pepper.

Place chicken on roasting rack** in roasting pan. Place the chicken in preheated oven for 10 minutes. Then reduce the heat to 225°F. Cover the chicken with a lid or foil. Continue to cook 3 to 4 hours longer. The internal temperature of the thickest part of the breast and thigh should reach 160°F, and the juices should run clear *(see sidebar on p. 41)*. Chicken should be golden brown.

Remove chicken to warmed platter, tented loosely with foil. Let stand 10 minutes. If you are serving the chicken hot, heat the pan juices to a boil; reduce by half. Serve as an accompaniment to the chicken.

Carve and serve immediately or refrigerate and serve chilled. Serve on a bed of parsley, surrounded with lemons.

Serves 3 to 4.

**Roasting should be done on a rack to keep meat up out of the juices during the cooking.

COOKING CLASS

TRUSSING POULTRY

Trussing a chicken helps to evenly distribute the heat during the cooking process, as well as maintaining the beautiful shape of the breast for presentation at the table.

Clean and dry the chicken. *Fold outer wing joint in towards back of chicken.*

Cut a piece of kitchen string about a yard long. *With chicken lying on its back, wrap center of string around legs twice to secure together. Run string under the tip of the breastbone to hold it in place, then pull string up either side of breast.*

Turn chicken over onto the breast side. Pull strings from front of chicken around to back, over the top of the wings. Tightly tie string together in center of back. Trim string ends.

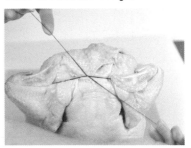

Place chicken on roasting rack.

CAPERS

"Capers" are the small green-gold buds of the caper bush, which grows around the Mediterranean Sea. Capers are usually pickled or packed in brine, but occasionally you will find them packed in salt. They come in sizes varying from $1/8$ inch to about $3/8$ inch. Larger "caper berries" are actually the berry produced when the bud of the caper bush is allowed to develop, then pickled and brined. They tend to be about the size of the tip of your little finger.

Because of the pickling, brining or salting, capers tend to be quite sour and salty, adding zing to sauces and dressings. They are a lovely complement to chicken, fish and veal dishes. You should taste them before using, to determine whether or not to rinse the capers before adding them to your dish.

Capers are sold in most supermarkets, found near the pickles and other condiments.

Sicilian Broccoli and Cauliflower Salad

Tender-crisp vegetables combined with tangy dressing, spicy olives, sweet peppers, and a zing of capers. For a more beautiful salad, I like to use flowerets only, no stems.

1 bunch broccoli cut bite size, about 1½ cups
½ head cauliflower cut bite size, about 2 cups
2 tablespoons red wine vinegar
¾ – 1 teaspoon salt
1 teaspoon oregano
¼ teaspoon freshly ground black pepper
⅓ cup extra-virgin olive oil
1 small red or yellow pepper, diced coarsely
½ red onion, very thinly sliced
12 large Sicilian olives, preferably green, pitted and
     coarsely chopped**
2 tablespoons capers, drained and rinsed

Steam broccoli and cauliflower until tender. Broccoli should be bright green. Remove from heat; refresh in ice water just until cool. Drain thoroughly.

Meanwhile combine vinegar, salt, oregano and pepper in large serving bowl. Whisk until salt is dissolved. Add oil in a steady stream, whisking constantly. *This dish can be prepared ahead to this point, storing vegetables and dressing separately in refrigerator. Allow dressing to come to room temperature before proceeding.*

Add drained vegetables to dressing, toss to coat. Add peppers, onions, olives and capers; toss again. Let stand, tossing frequently, at least 10 minutes. Serve within one hour, at room temperature.

Serves 4.

**To make HOT SPICY OLIVES, add 2 to 3 teaspoons of red pepper flakes to jar of olives, let marinate at least 24 hours.

Roasted Potato Salad

This salad is an explosion of flavors: the sweetness of the peppers, the tart and tangy dressing. Perfect for a picnic or Sunday dinner. Guaranteed to replace Grandma's as the family favorite!

for dressing :
1 – 2 teaspoons sugar
½ teaspoon salt
freshly ground pepper
2 tablespoons Dijon mustard
¼ cup red wine vinegar
½ cup olive oil

1 pound small red potatoes, scrubbed, dried, and quartered
1 tablespoon olive oil
salt and pepper
¼ red pepper
¼ yellow pepper
¼ green pepper
1 stalk celery, very thinly sliced
¼ red onion, medium diced
2 tablespoons snipped parsley
1 – 2 tablespoons snipped fresh dill (optional)

Prepare dressing: whisk sugar, salt, pepper, mustard and vinegar together until sugar and salt dissolve. Continue whisking, slowly adding olive oil. Set aside. *The dressing can be prepared one day in advance. Store at room temperature.*

Preheat oven to 450°F. Toss potatoes with olive oil, salt and pepper to taste. Spread potatoes and peppers on baking sheet lined with parchment. Roast until potatoes are browned on all edges, and skins on peppers are blistered, about 15 to 20 minutes. The potatoes should be soft in the center when pierced with a fork. Remove from oven. Transfer potatoes to large bowl. Wrap hot peppers in paper toweling to steam skins; leave until cool enough to handle, about 5 to 10 minutes. Use the toweling to rub off blackened skins, then chop peppers into ½-inch dice.

Toss potatoes with peppers, celery, and onion. Add dressing, parsley and dill; toss again. Serve warm, at room temperature, or chilled. Store in refrigerator. *This dish can be made ahead and refrigerated. Let stand at room temperature about 15 minutes before serving.*

Serves 4 to 6.

COOKING CLASS

FOOD SAFETY

Many summertime recipes are most flavorful at room temperature, which can be hazardous if proper care is not taken.

Germs like to grow in warm, moist places, between 45°F and 140°F, commonly known as the "**DANGER ZONE**." Most germs grow best between room temperature and body temperature. To keep germ growth to a minimum, food should be stored below 40°F, and optimally served cold, or heated to at least 165°F. If you plan to serve food at room temperature, it is imperative to serve it within two hours.

For safety's sake, any food that has been in the "**DANGER ZONE**" more than two hours should be discarded. It is important to understand that the two-hour rule is cumulative; if a food has been in the **DANGER ZONE** for one hour then refrigerated or heated, do not begin counting anew. If you are unsure how long a food has been in the **DANGER ZONE**, the rule is "When in doubt, throw it out!"

When making flaky pastry dough, the technique of "**cutting in**" the butter is common. It is easily accomplished:

Using a pastry cutter:
Add butter to dry ingredients, combine with dry ingredients with downward stokes, "cutting the butter" into small pieces with each stroke.

Using your hands:
Add butter to dry ingredients, rub the dry ingredients together with the butter, pinching the larger pieces, until desired consistency is reached.

Using a food processor:
With dry ingredients in workbowl, add butter. Using the steel knife, pulse 3 – 4 times, until desired consistency is reached. If using this method for pastry dough, I recommend adding the liquid by hand.

TIMESAVERS!

For a quick and easy, yet beautiful presentation for dessert, I often use purchased, prepared dessert sauces: chocolate, caramel, butterscotch.

THE RIGHT TOOL

At your local restaurant or beauty supply store, purchase some "squeezers." These are the tall, translucent, squeezable plastic bottles with cone-shaped tipped lids.

With the sauces in these bottles, you can create beautiful designs on plates, or merely drizzle the sauce over your finished dessert.

Chocolate Shortcakes

A classic mouth-watering dessert presentation, with a twist; showcasing the gorgeous fruits of summer! With all of that delicious fruit stacked inside maybe they should be called "chocolate tall cakes!" I suggest doubling the recipe, and freezing the cakes for a quick dessert later.

6 tablespoons sugar
1½ cups flour
6 tablespoons unsweetened cocoa
3 teaspoons baking powder
1 teaspoon baking soda
¼ teaspoon salt
2 ounces semi-sweet chocolate, finely chopped
6 tablespoons butter, at room temperature, cut in ½ inch cubes
¾ cup buttermilk
1 tablespoon sugar, for sprinkling

3 cups fresh berries, washed and dried
¼ – ½ cup sugar
1 cup whipping cream, whipped to soft peaks
½ cup purchased chocolate sauce for garnish
fresh mint leaves for garnish

Preheat oven to 450°F. Grease a small baking sheet or pan, set aside. Sift together sugar, flour, cocoa powder, baking powder, baking soda and salt. Add chocolate; stir to combine well. Cut in butter *(see sidebar)*, until mixture resembles coarse meal. Add buttermilk and work to combine. Do not overwork. The dough will be **very sticky**.

Turn dough out onto floured work surface. Pat into a rectangle 6" x 9" x ¾" thick. Use a knife to cut the rectangle into six 3" squares, or use a round cutter for 3" rounds or hearts. Transfer cakes to prepared baking sheet, sprinkle tops with one tablespoon sugar. Bake 8 to 10 minutes. Cool on wire rack. *The shortcakes can be made ahead and frozen at this point.*

Meanwhile, slice berries. Combine berries and sugar; check for sweetness. Add more sugar if necessary. Set aside up to 4 hours.

To assemble, split shortcakes in half widthwise. Place bottom half on serving plate, top with ¼ cup berry mixture. Replace top of shortcake. Garnish with dollop of whipping cream and ¼ cup berries. Lightly drizzle with chocolate sauce. Finish with fresh mint leaves.

Serves 6.

Casual Summer Evening

Marinated Shrimp

◆

"Fizzy" Lemonade

◆

Lemon Linguini
with
Fresh Tomato Sauce
and
Grilled Chicken

Italian Bread
(purchased)

◆

*Sauvignon Blanc or
Pinot Gris*

◆

Pear Sorbet

◆

Coffee or Tea

Casual Summer Evening

Three days ahead:
Prepare simple syrup for **"Fizzy Lemonade."** Refrigerate.
Fold the napkins if desired.

Two days ahead:
Shop for fresh fruits, vegetables and herbs, as well as fresh chicken breasts.
Cut and freeze pears for **Pear Sorbet** if you are using food processor method OR prepare pear sorbet mixture in blender; chill.

The day before:
Prepare **Marinated Shrimp**, cover and refrigerate.
Chill the wine, club soda for **"Fizzy Lemonade"** and other cold beverages.
Process frozen pears for **Pear Sorbet** if using food processor method OR freeze the chilled base in freezer or ice cream maker.
Put butter on its serving plate or bowl, cover and refrigerate.
Set up coffee or tea tray, after dinner drinks, glasses, etc.
Make ice.
Set the table. Put out any non-food items (salt and pepper, wine coaster, etc.)
Arrange the flowers.

The morning before:
Prepare garnish for **"Fizzy Lemonade."**
Cut vegetables for **Lemon Linguini.** Prepare the fresh tomato sauce, refrigerate. Prepare pepper strips for garnish.
Clean chicken breasts for **Lemon Linguini** if necessary. Place in resealable plastic bag, refrigerate.
Prepare marinade for chicken breasts, cover and set aside.
Set up coffee maker.

1 – 2 hours before guests arrive:
For **Lemon Linguini** add marinade to chicken breasts in bag; reseal, refrigerate for one hour.
Remove butter from refrigerator to soften.
Slice purchased bread, if serving.
After one hour, remove chicken breasts from marinade. Pat dry with paper towels, refrigerate until 15 minutes before cooking.
Remove fresh tomato sauce from refrigerator to come to room temperature.
Prepare lemon sauce for **Lemon Linguini**; cover and set aside.
Cook linguini, drain well and set aside *(see sidebar on p. 26).*
Grate Parmesan; cover and set aside.

Before your guests arrive:
Drain **Marinated Shrimp**, arrange on platter or in bowl with toothpicks for serving, chill until serving time.
Preheat the plates and platters as needed.
Heat a large pot of water to reheat the pasta, cover and keep hot.
Squeeze lemons and combine ingredients for **"Fizzy Lemonade."**

After the guests arrive:
Preheat grill or broiler for chicken, grill breasts and pepper strips.
Reheat the lemon sauce for **Lemon Linguini.**
Bring heated water to a boil, add cooked pasta. Allow the pasta to heat 30 seconds, drain well. Add to lemon sauce.
Plate **Lemon Linguini with Fresh Tomato Sauce and Grilled Chicken.**

Marinated Shrimp

A few tidbits to snack on while awaiting the main course, these shrimp are beautiful as well as enticing. The spices will awaken appetites, preparing your guests for what is yet to come.

half a small onion
half a carrot
half a celery stalk
2 teaspoons Old Bay seasoning or pickling spices
16 – 20 large shrimp, peeled and deveined, tails left on
    (see sidebar)

marinade:
2 tablespoons champagne vinegar or white wine vinegar
½ teaspoon salt
½ teaspoon celery salt
½ teaspoon hot pepper sauce
1 teaspoon mustard, preferably Dijon style
3 tablespoons olive oil
3 tablespoons vegetable oil

3 tablespoons minced parsley
3 tablespoons minced celery tops
1½ tablespoons capers, drained
¼ of a small red onion, minced
1 clove garlic, minced
½ teaspoon oregano
½ teaspoon thyme

In a medium saucepan, heat two quarts water to a boil with the onion, carrot, celery and the Old Bay seasoning. When water is boiling, add the shrimp. Bring back to a boil, then lower the heat to just below a simmer. There should appear only an occasional bubble. When shrimp are barely pink and opaque, pour out into strainer. Transfer shrimp into large glass bowl; discard the cooked vegetables.

Meanwhile, whisk vinegar, salts, pepper sauce and mustard until salt dissolves. Slowly add the olive and vegetable oils to create an emulsion *(see sidebar on p. 119)*. When all the oil has been added, taste, and correct the seasonings.

Pour marinade over hot cooked shrimp. Add remaining ingredients, toss. Cover and let marinate in refrigerator at least four hours, or overnight. Drain. Serve at room temperature, with toothpicks.

Serves 4.

TECHNIQUE

PEELING SHRIMP

Cleaning and peeling shrimp can be a tedious task. To accomplish it quickly you need the right tool. Use a shrimp deveiner, found at most supermarkets or seafood shops, or a pointed chopstick.

If the head is still attached remove it with a sharp knife.

Then, grasp the legs and pull them off.

Take the shrimp deveiner or chopstick and insert it under the shell from the head end of the shrimp down the back. It will pull away the shell and help to remove the black vein running down the back of the shrimp. Remove the tail if desired by pulling it off.

Rinse the shrimp under cold water.

"Fizzy" Lemonade

My family and I first learned about Meyer lemons while living in San Diego — we were lucky enough to have a Meyer lemon tree in our back yard! This refreshing libation is now a family staple. All other lemonades now receive constructive criticism from my discerning clan.

⅔ cup simple syrup (recipe below)
1 quart Club soda
½ cup freshly squeezed lemon juice (from 3 – 4 lemons)
freshly grated lemon zest of one or two lemons

for garnish: mint leaves, lemon slices, fresh strawberries or Maraschino cherries

Chill simple syrup and Club soda well. In large pitcher, pour lemon juice over ice. Add simple syrup, zest and Club soda. Stir to combine. Pour into tall glasses over ice. Garnish as desired.

Makes 4 servings.

Simple syrup:
½ cup sugar
½ cup water

Bring to boil, cool. Makes about ⅔ cup. Refrigerate to store. The syrup should keep approximately three weeks.

KNOW YOUR INGREDIENTS

LEMONS

Two varieties of lemons are most widely available in the marketplace: the Eureka and the Meyer.

Eureka lemons are more commonly found. They are characterized by their rather thick, bright yellow skins.

The skins of Meyer lemons are thinner, usually tinged with a bit of orange color. This is attributed to their heritage. They are a hybrid cross between lemons and Mandarin oranges or tangerines. Many people feel that Meyers are sweeter than Eureka lemons — this is due to their lower acidity. Meyers have a wonderful fruity, well-rounded flavor.

Lemon flavor comes not only from the juice but from the zest; the thin outer yellow portion of the rind, not the white pith underneath. Zest contains lemon oil, a powerful flavoring without the acidity of lemon juice. It is a flavoring of choice in many recipes. Use a fine grater to easily zest a lemon.

A medium lemon should yield about 2½ tablespoons of juice. Juicing can be made easier by microwaving a lemon on high for 10 seconds, then rolling on a hard surface before juicing.

Lemons can be stored at room temperature for two or three days, but beyond that they should be refrigerated.

Each part of this recipe can stand on its own, or in different combinations. For example:

For a quick, light summer meal; serve the tomato sauce on fully cooked angel hair, top with freshly grated Parmesan.

Serve the grilled chicken breast on its own, or topped with a few tablespoons of the tomato sauce for a light entree.

Or make **bruschetta**:

Brush slices of Italian bread with olive oil and toast on a heated barbecue grill or grill pan, or under a heated broiler. Top with drained tomato sauce, serve immediately as an appetizer or hors d'oeurve.

COOKING CLASS

PERFECT PASTA EVERY TIME

How long should you cook pasta? The Italians say "al dente," which means "to the teeth." Perfectly cooked pasta should be chewy; not mushy, but firm to the bite. For perfect results, timing can be critical, so check the package — the manufacturer will tell you.

The sauce can almost always cook a few extra minutes if necessary, but not the pasta. What to do if your pasta is ready before you are? Remove the pasta from the water and drain well. Keep the remaining pasta water simmering, and when you are ready simply reheat the pasta by either pouring the hot water over the pasta, or immersing the pasta in the hot water for 20 to 30 seconds. As always, drain well.

Avoid cooking pasta in too little water, overcooking the pasta, and over-saucing the pasta. Remember, the dish is primarily about the pasta, not the sauce.

Lemon Linguini with Fresh Tomato Sauce and Grilled Chicken

The fresh aroma of basil, tomatoes and garlic will entice you. And the perfect combination of succulent chicken, sweet tomatoes, intense lemon and nutty Parmesan will capture you.

For sauce:
3 cups plum tomatoes, washed, cored, seeded if desired, and cut into thin wedges
1 teaspoon salt
25 fresh basil leaves cut in chiffonade *(see sidebar on p. 39)*, or 2 teaspoons dried basil
2 tablespoons snipped Italian or flat-leafed parsley
2 cloves garlic, minced
juice of 1 lemon, freshly squeezed
pepper, to taste
2 tablespoons olive oil

For chicken:
3 tablespoons Kosher salt
2 cloves garlic, minced
juice of 1 lemon, freshly squeezed
1 teaspoon dried oregano
4 skinless, boneless chicken breast halves
12 very thin strips of red or yellow bell pepper, for garnish
1 recipe Lemon Linguini *(see recipe on following page)*

Place tomatoes in large bowl, sprinkle with salt, basil, parsley, garlic, lemon juice and pepper. Stir gently just to mix. Drizzle olive oil over, toss again and set aside to marinate for at least one hour or as many as six. Stir occasionally.

For marinade, dissolve Kosher salt in ½ cup warm water. Add ½ cup cold water, garlic, lemon juice and oregano. Place chicken breasts in resealable plastic bag; add marinade. Seal and refrigerate for one hour. Remove chicken from marinade, pat dry. *Chicken may be prepared 6 hours ahead to this point. Cover and refrigerate. Bring to room temperature to continue.*

Preheat grill or broiler. Grill chicken breasts and pepper strips over hot coals, or broil under preheated broiler. Cook 7 to 10 minutes, turning occasionally as necessary, taking care not to overcook. Remove from heat, diagonally slice chicken breasts, keeping each intact. Keep warm. Meanwhile, prepare Lemon Linguini.

Divide lemon linguini among four serving plates. Top each serving with layer of fresh tomato sauce, then sliced chicken breast. Garnish with pepper strips; sprinkle with Parmesan.

Serves 4.

Lemon Linguini

Excite and luxuriate your taste buds with the freshness of lemon, and the smooth silkiness of cream!

2 tablespoons butter
1 cup heavy cream**
freshly grated zest of two lemons
juice of two freshly squeezed lemons
¾ cup freshly grated Parmesan cheese
8 – 12 ounces linguini, cooked according to package directions

Over high heat, combine butter and cream in large non-reactive skillet *(see sidebar on p. 55)*. When cream begins to boil, add lemon juice and grated peel, stir thoroughly. Cook and stir over high heat until the sauce is slightly thickened and lightly coats a spoon. *At this point you can put the sauce on hold for an hour, simply remove it from the heat and cover. Gently reheat before assembling dish.*

Meanwhile, cook linguini in boiling water until al dente, drain. To assemble dish, toss hot drained pasta and half of Parmesan with lemon sauce. Serve with remaining Parmesan sprinkled on top.

Serves 4.

**Low-Fat Version:*

For the lemon sauce, substitute 1 cup low-fat or non-fat sour cream for the heavy cream. Use only 1 tablespoon butter. Melt butter in non-reactive skillet, then add lemon juice and zest. Boil over high heat until lemon juice is reduced by half. Remove from heat, cool slightly. Stir in sour cream, thinning with a little hot pasta water if desired. Keep warm, but DO NOT OVERHEAT!! Toss with hot cooked pasta; continue recipe as directed.

This lemon linguini is also a great dish to stand on its own as a side for an entrée, or prepare the lemon sauce and serve it tossed with a stuffed pasta such as ravioli or tortellini.

KNOW YOUR INGREDIENTS

Freshly squeezed lemon juice is like no other — it has the wonderful clean, clear, fresh taste and aroma of lemons. Recipes call for the freshly squeezed stuff because it is far superior. After only half an hour fresh juice begins to deteriorate, and the flavor loss is noticeable. Try a side-by-side comparison.

The flavor is preserved if frozen immediately, so if you have a lot of lemons, give it a try. I like to freeze mine in an ice cube tray, then store the cubes in a resealable plastic bag. One large lemon yields about 3 tablespoons of juice.

If you must buy bottled lemon juice, I recommend the frozen product. To me the bottled kind off the shelf tastes like chemicals.

Freshly grated zest is described as the very thin colored outer peel of the citrus; not the inner, white pith, which can be bitter. It imparts much more citrus flavor to foods, but none of the sourness of the juice, because of the essential oils contained only in the outer skin. These oils tend to dry out easily, so the zest should be used while it is fresh.

Fine thin strips of zest used for garnish can be made with a bar tool called a "zester." Larger quantities are more easily obtained with a fine grater, or by first removing the thin peel with a sharp knife, then chopping the peel with sugar in a food processor.

Poire William is a clear brandy made by distilling fermented pear juice. It has a very strong pear aroma and flavor, so it adds to the wonderful flavor of the pears in this sorbet. The alcohol content will keep the sorbet a bit soft, for easier scooping.

Although Poire William usually comes from Switzerland, it is described as **eau-de-vie** (oh-deuh-vee), which is French for "water of life." Other common fruit eaux-de-vie include Kirsch (cherry brandy), and Framboise (raspberry brandy).

Many sorbet recipes call for alcohol, because it is important in crystallization. Alcohol has a lower freezing point than water, thus it causes slower freezing, and produces finer crystals, for a smoother, slushier sorbet. Without alcohol, ice chunks tend to form.

The alcohol is also an important flavor component, dissolving some flavors that will not dissolve in water, giving a more well-rounded, complex flavor to the finished dish.

Poire William is expensive, but you will make this dish again and again once you try it.

Pear Sorbet

Very refreshing and elegant, this cool dessert cannot possibly get any easier to prepare. And it always gets rave reviews!

1 (15-¼ ounce) can of pears in heavy syrup
   (halves, slices, or diced) chilled very cold
¼ to ½ cup sugar
1 teaspoon freshly squeezed lemon juice
2 – 3 tablespoons Poire William (pear brandy)

In food processor: (allow 4 to 6 hours to freeze)

Stir together pears, syrup, sugar, lemon juice and brandy in shallow freezer dish. Roughly chop pears if they are in large pieces. Freeze until firm, about 4 to 6 hours.

Scoop pear mixture into food processor and process until the consistency is like snow. Return to freezer to store, or serve immediately.

OR in blender: (allow 3 to 5 hours to freeze)

Combine pears, syrup, sugar, lemon juice and brandy in blender jar. Puree until smooth. Pour into shallow pan. Place pan in freezer. When ice crystals begin to form around the edges of the pan, stir the mixture with a wire whisk. Continue to freeze, stirring the mixture every half an hour until mixture becomes the consistency of snow. Store in freezer.

OR in ice cream freezer: (allow 15 to 30 minutes to freeze)

Combine pears, syrup, sugar, lemon juice and brandy in blender jar. Puree until smooth. Chill well. Pour cold mixture into ice cream freezer; freeze according to manufacturer's directions.

Makes about 2 cups. Serves 4 to 6.

Variations:

*Substitute Mandarin oranges and orange liqueur, or
Peaches and Peach Schnapps, or
Pineapple and coconut rum (Malibu).*

Moonlight Summer Solstice Supper

Figs & Goat Cheese

◆

Scallops
With
Pink Grapefruit Sauce

Seasoned Rice
(optional)

Zucchini Ribbons
(optional, see p. 53 for recipe)

French Bread
(purchased)

◆

Sauvignon Blanc

◆

Peaches in Champagne

◆

Coffee or Tea

Moonlight Summer Solstice Supper

Three days ahead:
Fold the napkins if desired.

The day before:
Shop for fruit, vegetables and scallops.
Prepare **Pink Grapefruit Sauce** for the scallops. Cover and refrigerate.
Wash and cut **Zucchini Ribbons**, wrap and refrigerate (see recipe on p. 53).
Put butter on its serving plate or bowl, cover and refrigerate.
Chill the wine and other cold beverages.
Set up coffee or tea tray, after dinner drinks, glasses, etc.
Make ice.
Set the table. Put out any non-food items (salt and pepper, wine coaster, etc.)
Arrange the flowers.

The morning before:
Cut grapefruit into supremes for **Scallops with Pink Grapefruit Sauce**. Cover and refrigerate.
Prepare **Figs & Goat Cheese**: line platter with greens, cut figs, slice cheese, arrange atop. Cover and refrigerate.
Set up coffee maker.

6 hours before guests arrive:
Wash and drain scallops. Prepare brine mixture, brine scallops 30 minutes. Remove from bag, pat dry.
Wrap scallops with prosciutto; refrigerate.

3 hours before guests arrive:
Peel and slice peaches for **Peaches in Champagne**. Pour Champagne over peaches, cover and refrigerate.

1 – 2 hours before guests arrive:
Prepare the **Seasoned Rice**, tent and keep warm in 160° oven.
Remove butter from refrigerator to soften.
Slice purchased bread, if serving.

Before your guests arrive:
Preheat the plates and platters as needed.
Place platter of **Figs and Goat Cheese** on serving table.

After the guests arrive:
Remove scallops from refrigerator 15 minutes prior to cooking to allow to come to room temperature.
Reheat the **Pink Grapefruit Sauce**; swirl in butter and Cointreau.
Sauté the **Zucchini Ribbons**.
Sauté the scallops, plate and serve on warmed plates.
Transfer the **Peaches in Champagne** to serving dishes, garnish.

FRESH FIGS

Most figs are grown around the Mediterranean or in California. Common varieties which are available fresh during the summer months include:

Mission or "Black Mission" figs have dark purplish-black skins and pink flesh.

Brown Turkey figs have brownish-purple skins and rich red flesh.

Adriatic figs are green skinned with white flesh.

Celeste figs are slightly larger, purple skinned with rose-colored flesh.

Kadota figs tend to have thicker yellow-green skins and violet colored flesh.

Ripe figs should feel slightly soft, with smooth skins.

Store fresh figs refrigerated for no longer than 2 to 3 days as they are highly perishable.

To slice figs more easily, chill in refrigerator for 1 to 2 hours before cutting.

Figs and Goat Cheese

An unusual salad showcasing fresh figs. I like to use a combination of two different varieties of figs for contrast against the dark salad greens and the ivory cheese. The sweetness of the figs is a wonderful accompaniment to the creamy, salty cheese.

dark green salad greens
4 fresh figs
3 ounces fresh goat cheese, sliced
1 tablespoon fresh parsley, leaves separated
freshly ground black pepper, to taste

Wash, dry and trim salad greens. Spread greens over a serving platter. Slice unpeeled figs into thin wedges from top to bottom. Arrange atop salad greens with the goat cheese slices. Sprinkle parsley leaves and freshly ground black pepper over platter to garnish. Serve at room temperature.

Serves 4.

Peaches in Champagne

I grew up near peach country in Utah. Late in the summer we would go to the peach festival. It was always a very special time, riding the Ferris wheel with my dad. This recipe brings back those memories. For a dramatic presentation, serve the peaches in stemmed glasses.

4 large ripe Freestone peaches
1 – 2 tablespoons sugar
1 cup Champagne
fresh mint sprigs, for garnish

Peel and pit peaches. Slice thinly into a large bowl, catching any juices that drip. Sprinkle with the sugar if desired. Pour Champagne over peaches, gently stir to coat. Allow fruit to marinate for one hour in refrigerator. *If you prefer to make this recipe ahead up to 4 hours, you will need to completely cover the fruit with Champagne to prevent browning of the peaches.*

To serve, spoon the peaches into serving dishes, drizzle the juices from the bowl over the fruit. Garnish with fresh mint.

Variation:
For a slightly heavier desert, replace the Champagne with Port or Cabernet Sauvignon.

TECHNIQUE

PEELING AND PITTING PEACHES

To peel peaches quickly and easily, you will need a saucepan of boiling water and a bowl of ice water, each deep enough to cover a peach.

With a sharp knife make an "X" in the bottom of each peach, just piercing the skin.

Using a slotted spoon, gently lower a peach into the boiling water for 45 seconds to a minute. Remove the peach; plunge instantly into the ice water. Let stand about 1 minute longer.

Remove the peach from the ice water, and slip away the peel starting at the "X" on the bottom.

To pit the peach, run the knife down the seam of the peach to the pit. Continue all the way around the fruit, connecting the cut.

Grasp each side of the peach and twist in opposite directions. The pit will release itself on one side. Either pry the pit away from the other side, or simply slice the peach away from the remaining pit. Freestone peaches will release the pit much more easily than cling peaches.

Scallops with Pink Grapefruit Sauce

for sauce:
2 teaspoons butter
1 shallot, finely minced
½ teaspoon dried thyme
salt, to taste
½ cup medium dry white wine
1 cup freshly squeezed pink grapefruit juice
(from about 3 or 4 grapefruits)
½ teaspoon finely grated grapefruit zest
sugar to taste
½ teaspoon arrowroot or cornstarch
1 – 2 tablespoons grapefruit juice, wine or water

24 large sea scallops
¼ cup sugar
2½ tablespoons kosher salt

6 slices prosciutto
3 – 4 tablespoons corn oil, for sautéing

to finish:
2 teaspoons butter
1 teaspoon Cointreau
2 fresh pink grapefruits cut into supremes
Seasoned Rice *(see sidebar at right)*
Zucchini Ribbons *(see recipe on p. 53)*

To make the sauce: in non-reactive pan, melt butter over medium heat. Add shallots and thyme, sprinkle with salt. Sauté until shallots are translucent, but not brown. Add wine, raise heat to boil. Reduce mixture by half. Measure 1 tablespoon grapefruit juice into a small bowl, set aside. Add remaining juice and zest to wine; continue boiling until mixture is reduced to ½ cup. Add sugar to taste. Stir arrowroot or cornstarch into the reserved 1 tablespoon grapefruit juice; add to sauce, bring to boil. Keep warm. *The sauce can be prepared to this point one day in advance. Refrigerate sauce; reheat to continue.*

TECHNIQUE

CITRUS SUPREMES

Cutting citrus fruits into **supremes** *is an easy task, and makes for a beautiful presentation.*

First, slice both top and bottom from the fruit, creating a flat surface and revealing plenty of the inner fruit.

Stand the fruit on one of the cut ends. Then slowly, with a thin sharp knife, cut away the sides of the rind, again exposing the fruit.

When the fruit is completely peeled, hold it in your hand over a bowl to catch the juices. Slice toward the center of the fruit on either side of each membrane, releasing the fruit supreme. This can be done one day ahead. Cover and refrigerate.

Wash scallops, drain. Dissolve sugar and kosher salt in ½ cup hot water. Add 1½ cups cold water, pour into large resealable plastic bag with the scallops. Seal and set aside for 20 minutes. Remove scallops from brine, pat dry.

With a very sharp knife, cut each slice of prosciutto into four lengthwise strips. Wrap the edge of each scallop with a strip of prosciutto, leaving flat sides of scallops exposed; secure with toothpick if necessary. *The scallops can be prepared 6 hours in advance to this point. Cover and chill until ready to cook. Let stand 10 minutes to come to room temperature before proceeding.*

Heat oil in large sauté pan over medium high heat. Pat scallops dry if necessary. Cook scallops until lightly browned, about 2 minutes on each side. Remove from pan.

Swirl remaining butter and Cointreau into warm sauce. Puddle on dinner plate, top with hot scallops and grapefruit supremes. Serve with "Seasoned Rice" and zucchini ribbons.

Serves 4.

EXTRA TOUCHES

SEASONED RICE

1 cup long grain rice (200 g.)
    (converted is OK, DO NOT
    use instant)
1 teaspoon salt, divided
2 tablespoons rice vinegar
2 teaspoons sugar

In large pot, heat 1½ to 2 quarts or liters of water to boiling. Add ½ teaspoon salt and the rice, stir. Boil 13 to 14 minutes, until rice is tender. Drain in sieve or colander. Immediately transfer to a heatproof serving dish; toss with remaining salt, vinegar and sugar. Cover with foil, leaving a vent for steam to escape. You do not want the rice to steam. Place in preheated 160°F oven to hold, for up to two hours. Stir before serving.

Makes 3 cups cooked rice, serves 4.

Sumptuous Summer Fete

Caramelized Almond Roasted Dates

Champagne

◆

Tomato Basil Soup

Sauvignon Blanc

◆

Marinated "London Broil"

Vegetables with Capers
and
Rosemary Potatoes

Assorted Breads
(purchased)
and
Flavored Butter
(optional, see recipes in
"Show-Offs!!" section)

*Pinot Noir or
Cabernet Sauvignon*

◆

R.S.V.P. Fruit Plate

◆

Coffee or Tea

Sumptuous Summer Fete

Three days ahead:
Caramelize almonds and pit dates for **Caramelized Almond Roasted Dates.**
Chop vegetables for **Tomato and Basil Soup**. Store in plastic bag and refrigerate.
Trim, wash and steam vegetables for **Vegetables with Capers**. Wrap in plastic and refrigerate.
Prepare dressing for **Vegetables with Capers**. Cover and refrigerate.
Prepare **Creme Fraiche** if desired, set aside.
Prepare flavored butters, if desired. Cover and refrigerate.
Fold the napkins if desired.

Two days ahead:
Prepare **Tomato Basil Soup**; cover and refrigerate. Prepare croutons if serving hot; store in airtight container.
Prepare sour cream sauce for **RSVP Fruit Plate**. Cover and refrigerate.

The day before:
Stuff and wrap dates with prosciutto. Cover and refrigerate.
Shop for fresh fruit for **RSVP Fruit Plate.**
Trim and score the steak for **London Broil.**
Prepare the marinade for **London Broil**; begin marinating the meat in plastic resealable bag in refrigerator.
Put the flavored butter on its serving plate or bowl, cover and refrigerate.
Chill the wine and other cold beverages.
Set up coffee or tea tray, after dinner drinks, glasses, etc.
Make ice.
Set the table. Put out any non-food items (salt and pepper, wine coaster, etc.)
Arrange the flowers.

The morning before:
Prepare lemon garnish if desired and basil chiffonade for **Tomato Basil Soup**. Store in airtight containers and refrigerate.
Wash and cut potatoes for **Rosemary Potatoes**. Toss with oil, herbs and pepper. DO NOT SALT
    (this should be done just before the potatoes are put into the oven). Cover and refrigerate.
Wash and dry fruit for **RSVP Fruit Plate**; store in airtight container in refrigerator.
Prepare strawberry fans and mint garnish, cover and refrigerate.
Set up coffee maker.

1 – 2 hours before guests arrive:
Finish the **Vegetables with Capers** by tossing vegetables with dressing; arrange on platter. Cover and set aside to come
    to room temperature.
Remove **London Broil** steak from marinade, pat dry to cook. Allow ½ hour to come to room temperature before
    cooking. Prepare red wine sauce; chill.
Remove butter from refrigerator to soften.
Slice purchased bread, if serving.
Sauce plates for **RSVP Fruit Plates** and arrange fruit on top. Sprinkle with sugar mixture; refrigerate.
Roast dates, place on serving dish.

Before your guests arrive:
Prepare and preheat the grill for the **London Broil.**
Reheat the **Tomato and Basil Soup** if serving hot.
Preheat the plates and platters as needed.

After the guests arrive:
Plate and garnish the soup.
Salt and roast the potatoes.
Grill or broil the **London Broil**. Reheat the wine sauce.
Broil **RSVP Fruit Plates** just before serving; garnish with mint.

Caramelized Almond Roasted Dates

The flavors of these dates are perfectly balanced: the sweetness of the dates, the slightly bitter caramel, the saltiness of the prosciutto. Serve these tantalizing tidbits with cocktails before dinner. But I warn you, they are addictive.

16 large whole almonds
1 tablespoon sugar
16 large dried dates
4 thin slices prosciutto

Place almonds and sugar in small skillet. Cook over high heat until sugar melts and coats nuts. Continue cooking until sugar turns light caramel color. Immediately spread and separate nuts onto a baking sheet to cool.

Pit any unpitted dates by making a small lengthwise slice in the fruit and pulling out the long narrow seed. *The almonds and dates can be prepared up to three days in advance to this point. Seal in separate airtight containers. Store at room temperature.*

Stuff a caramelized almond into the cavity left from the pit in each date.

Cut each slice of prosciutto in half crosswise, then lengthwise to make a total of 16 small rectangular pieces. Starting at the short side of the rectangle, roll each date in a prosciutto piece, wrapping tightly. Place dates on a parchment lined baking sheet. *Can prepare ahead to this point one day in advance. Cover and refrigerate until ready to cook.*

Preheat oven to 350°F. Roast dates until prosciutto begins to crisp, 4 to 6 minutes. Watch carefully, as the dates burn very quickly. Remove from oven. Allow to cool. Serve on a platter.

Serves 4 as an appetizer.

DATES

Dates grow in hot dessert climates in the California and Arizona desserts as well as in North Africa and the Middle East.

Choose dates that are plump and soft, with a smooth shiny appearance.

Store them tightly wrapped at room temperature for up to six months.

Packaged dates, both pitted and unpitted are available year-round in the produce section of your super-market or at Mediterranean specialty stores.

Tomato Basil Soup

One hot summer I planted too many successful tomato plants. Each afternoon, I would go out to my garden and harvest the beautiful red, warm tomatoes. I could never resist just biting into one, letting the juice explode in my mouth. For me, it was the essence of summer. This soup captures that flavor. Italian or plum tomatoes are best for this recipe, as they are meatier.

2 teaspoons butter
2 tablespoons minced onion
1 tablespoon minced carrot
1 clove garlic, minced
1 (15-ounce) can of tomatoes, or
    1 pound ripe tomatoes, peeled, cored, chopped
1 cup good quality chicken or vegetable stock
8 fresh basil leaves, cut in chiffonade, divided *(see sidebar)*
croutons *(see side bar for recipe),* or lemon slices
1 tablespoon freshly grated Parmesan cheese

In medium saucepan over medium heat, heat butter until sizzling, add onion, carrot and garlic. Cook until onion is translucent, but not brown, about 4 minutes. Add tomatoes, and half of basil; continue cooking 15 to 20 minutes longer until tomatoes are very soft. If tomatoes become too dry, add a little of the stock to moisten. Allow to cool briefly.

Transfer the mixture to a blender in small batches, taking care to fill blender jar no more than half full. Personal experience has taught me that hot liquids tend to "blow up" in the blender if it is filled too full or started at high speed. Hold the lid on the blender jar tightly with a potholder or kitchen towel, THEN turn on blender, starting at low speed. Increase speed to puree the soup until smooth. Strain soup through a sieve.** Add any remaining stock. *The soup can be made 2 days ahead to this point. Refrigerate, or freeze for 4 months.*

Return to heat. Heat through, correct seasoning. Add remaining half of basil. Ladle the soup into serving bowls. Serve hot with croutons floating on top and a sprinkling of Parmesan; or chilled with a slice of lemon floating on top.

Makes about three cups soup; for 4 to 6 appetizer portions or 2 to 3 main courses.

**Passing soups and sauces through a sieve creates a silky smooth, fine textured result. The finer the sieve, the smoother the result. Most kitchens have a coarse mesh sieve of some kind. You may want to invest in a fine mesh sieve for velvety smooth sauces and soups.

TECHNIQUE

*Cutting basil into **chiffonade**:*

Wash and dry leaves, stack.

Roll the stack from side to side, like a cigar.

Cut in thin strips with a scissors or knife.

EXTRA TOUCHES

MAKE YOUR OWN CROUTONS

You will need thin slices of bread, with crust on if using a baguette, or cutouts of sandwich bread, and butter.

Arrange bread slices on baking sheet; toast one side under broiler. Turn slices over, spread with butter, toast buttered side. Can be made ahead 2 days, then stored in an airtight container.

Removing the silvery membrane from the meat.

"Scoring" a steak:
The slits create more surface area, allowing more of the marinade to be absorbed.

Horizontal slits: using the tip of a knife, make small cuts all the way through the meat, across the grain in parallel pattern on one side.

Vertical slits: Turn steak over, "score" in parallel lines with the grain of the meat on the other side.

COOKING CLASS

*Whether broiling, grilling, sautéing or roasting, foods should be **patted dry** before cooking. Moisture will create steam; we want dry heat to create that brown crust. Also remember that the food should be at **room temperature** before cooking.*

Marinated "London Broil"

This recipe is a consistent satisfying favorite—for my cooking classes, family dinners or entertaining. I'm not sure whether it is the tender. juicy meat, or the "to die for" sauce that trips everyone's switch. But the reaction is always "OH, baby, oh!"

2 pounds flank steak, or London broil

For marinade:
⅓ cup minced shallots, or garlic
3 tablespoons soy sauce
¼ cup olive oil
3 tablespoons fresh rosemary or thyme
(If using rosemary, I prefer to use only fresh, as the dried herb is too hard, and feels like needles in my mouth!)
½ teaspoon Tabasco sauce
3 tablespoons red wine vinegar

For optional sauce:
reserved marinade, from meat
½ cup red wine, optional (I recommend Pinot Noir or Cabernet Sauvignon)
3 tablespoons unsalted butter, in 3 pieces

Trim membrane and fat from the steak, and then "score" the steak as directed in the sidebar at left. Mix marinade ingredients in shallow dish or large resealable plastic bag. Place steak in dish or bag, cover or seal bag, squeezing out as much air as possible. Marinate steak for 2 to 24 hours, turning steak and spreading marinade over at least three times during the marinating process. Bring steak to room temperature before cooking.

Preheat grill or broiler. Reserving marinade, remove steak from marinade, **pat dry**. Place steak on grill or under broiler at the distance from heat and for times provided in the chart at the end of this recipe. Turn every 2 to 3 minutes to help keep the meat tender. Remove to warmed platter, tent with foil, let stand 4 to 5 minutes.

Meanwhile, in a non-reactive pan** bring marinade to the boil, adding wine if desired. Boil at least 5 minutes to destroy any pathogens from the raw meat. Reduce slightly. Remove the sauce from heat; whisk in butter one tablespoon at a time, until melted and sauce thickens slightly. Keep sauce warm.

Carve meat in thin diagonal slices across the grain of the meat. Arrange slices on warmed platter; drizzle sauce over meat. Garnish with parsley, or surround with vegetables.

Serves 6.

Note: Any leftover meat makes a fantastic sandwich filling or a great topper for a hearty salad!

Grilling/Broiling temperatures for London Broil:

Thickness	Inches from Heat source*	RARE	MEDIUM	WELL-DONE
½ – ¾"	1 inch	3 – 4min/side	4 – 5min/side	6 min/side
1 inch	2 inches	4 – 5min/side	6 – 7min/side	8 min/side
1½"	3 inches	5 – 6 min/side	7 – 8 min/side	9 – 10 min/side
2 inches	4 inches	6-7 min/side	8 – 9 min/side	11 – 13 min/side
Internal temp.		(120 – 140°F)	(145 – 155°F)	(160 – 180°F)

Measurements are from the flame or heat source to the surface of the food.

Cooking times are approximate, and will vary with the temperature of the heat source.

**A non-reactive pan is one that will not react with the acids in foods. Therefore, it must be made of stainless steel, tin, or glass, or lined with non-stick, enamel or porcelain. Do not use cast iron or aluminum when cooking acidic foods, such as tomatoes, citrus, wine or vinegar, as the metal pan can react with these types of foods, altering their flavor and color.*

THE RIGHT TOOLS

INSTANT-READ THERMOMETERS

An instant-read meat thermometer is an invaluable tool in any kitchen and can be used for cooking more than just meats. The smaller instant-read types are typically more accurate than a larger, traditional meat thermometer, registering temperature in a matter of seconds, and leaving a smaller hole in the meat. So, the thinner the probe, the better. Another advantage is that you can test the meat in more than one place.

When purchasing an instant-read thermometer, you should look for one that is easily read. A digital type is more exact and more expensive than a dial face. Digital thermometers require batteries; dial face units do not.

When using an instant-read thermometer, you should test the thickest part of the food. Since the center of the thickest section is farthest away from the heat source, it will be the last to cook. Make sure that the sensors are fully inserted into the food. The sensors in a dial face thermometer are about 1 to 1½ inches from the tip, as compared to the sensors in the tip of a digital thermometer. That means if you are using a dial face thermometer, it must be inserted at least 1½ inches. If you are testing a steak or a chicken breast that is less than 1½ inches thick, you should insert the thermometer into the food from the side, so that it will penetrate far enough for an accurate reading. Avoid placing the probe near or on a bone, as it will distort your temperature reading.

Be sure to clean your thermometer thoroughly after each use. You can regularly test the accuracy of your thermometer by placing the probe into boiling water. At sea level, it should register 212°F.

Rosemary Potatoes

All warm and golden, crisp on the outside, tender and moist on the inside, the aroma filling the kitchen, these potatoes are comfort food and a family favorite in our home.

1½ pounds small new potatoes, scrubbed, dried
1 – 2 tablespoons olive oil
2 – 3 tablespoons fresh rosemary, snipped**
2 – 3 tablespoons Italian parsley, snipped
salt and pepper to taste

Preheat oven to 425°F. Line a large baking sheet with parchment paper. If necessary, halve or quarter any potatoes that are too large to be "bite size." All of the potatoes or pieces should be about the same size, to ensure even cooking.

In a bowl, toss potatoes with oil, add herbs, garlic, salt and pepper to taste, combine well. *If you need to put this dish on hold, do not add salt, cover and hold up to three hours. Salt before continuing.*

Roast potatoes in preheated oven 20 to 35 minutes depending on the size of the potatoes. The potatoes should be soft in the center when tested with a fork. Serve hot or at room temperature.

Serves 4 to 6.

**I don't recommend dried rosemary in this dish, as it seems "needle-like" and doesn't soften in the cooking process.

You may want to add additional herbs if desired or substitute sage in place of the rosemary for a different flavor.

Or try substituting half sweet potatoes, cut to size, for half of the new potatoes!

TIMESAVERS!

Parchment paper or cooking parchment can be found in many supermarkets or kitchenware shops. It comes in rolls or in sheets.

It is invaluable in this recipe to prevent the potatoes from sticking, even with LOTS of oil in the pan. You may find that you use it for quite a number of other dishes when you see how easy clean up becomes.

Vegetables with Capers

The combination of the tart, saltiness of the capers and the sweetness of the different colored vegetables, the bite of the garlic, and the freshness of the herbs create a dramatic presentation to compliment a myriad of dishes. A very versatile and unique dish easily transported for a picnic, yet elegant enough for a sophisticated dinner party.

1 pound choice young carrots, green beans, asparagus, broccoli, or cauliflower
salt for cooking the vegetables *(see sidebar)*
3 tablespoons extra-virgin olive oil
1 or 2 cloves garlic
2 tablespoons chopped parsley
⅛ teaspoon salt
freshly ground pepper, to taste
2 teaspoons capers,** drained and rinsed

Peel or scrape carrots or asparagus, trim and wash your choice of vegetables. If you have chosen a variety of vegetables, cook each type separately. For each type, add vegetables to boiling salted water, or steam, until just barely tender. Place cooked, drained vegetables immediately into cold water bath to stop cooking process. Let cool 4 to 5 minutes; drain well. *This can be done up to 4 days in advance. Refrigerate vegetables until one hour before serving time; proceed.*

For dressing, chop garlic, parsley and 1 teaspoon capers in food processor, or by hand, until finely minced. Add olive oil, salt and pepper, blend. Stir in remaining capers. Set aside in small jar. *Will keep up to two weeks in refrigerator. Bring to room temperature and whisk to restore consistency before serving.* This may seem like a small amount of dressing, but it will be enough!

To serve: Toss vegetables with dressing, arrange on platter. Serve at room temperature.

Serves 4 to 6.

**Capers are small berry-like buds varying in size from that of a small pea to as large as the tip of your little finger. Their distinctive, sharp flavor can add a lovely compliment to sauces and dressings. You will find them in the condiment section of your supermarket. For more information, see the sidebar on page 18.

TIME SAVERS!

COOKING VEGETABLES IN ADVANCE.

Here's a little trick from the catering trade:

Wash, trim and prepare vegetables for cooking.

For boiling vegetables, bring a pot of water to a boil; add vegetables and 1 teaspoon salt per quart to a pot of water AFTER the water comes to a boil. Salt is important to maintain the color of the vegetables. Cook until barely tender. Remove from heat; drain. Refresh.

Or steam vegetables in a vegetable steamer until barely tender. Remove from heat; drain. Refresh.

To refresh vegetables: immediately plunge vegetables in bowl of ice water to cool quickly and stop the cooking process. This will help to maintain the color and crispness of the vegetables. Remove vegetables from the ice bath in 4 to 5 minutes. Drain well. Wrap in paper towel or tea towel, then in plastic. Refrigerate up to 4 days.

To serve:

Toss with a dressing, or quickly reheat in microwave or saucepan with melted butter.

COOKING CLASS

BE KIND TO YOUR POTS

To avoid pitting the bottom of your pan, wait until the water is boiling before adding the salt. The salt will dissolve more quickly, and be distributed in the water by the bubbles.

Making **strawberry fans**:
Keep the green bit on top for color.

Cut slices in berry leaving a small bit attached at the top.

Press and fan out.

R.S.V.P. Summer Fruit Plate

The hot, crunchy topping is cooled by the fruits and sauce. A very simple but beautiful dessert, showing off the finest of summer fruit flavors and colors.

½ cup regular or non-fat sour cream,
    or crème fraiche *(see sidebar on p. 107)*
4 teaspoons confectioner's sugar
1 teaspoon freshly squeezed lemon juice
1 – 2 tablespoons milk
½ cup blueberries, washed and dried
8 strawberries, washed, dried, fanned
½ cup raspberries, washed and dried
½ cup blackberries, washed and dried
½ cup white grapes, washed and dried
2 tablespoons brown sugar
1 – 2 teaspoons butter, softened
mint sprigs, for garnish

Mix sour cream, confectioner's sugar and lemon juice, thin with milk if necessary. The sauce should be the consistency of thick cream. Spoon onto center of four ovenproof dessert plates in "puddles." Arrange fruit on top.

In a small bowl, mash brown sugar and butter together with a fork to combine. Sprinkle over fruit. *If necessary, this dish can be put on hold here. Prepare to this point as much as three hours in advance. Refrigerate prepared fruit plates and topping until serving time, continue.*

Preheat broiler. Broil 1 to 2 minutes, until butter and sugar sizzle. Garnish with fresh mint; serve immediately.

Serves 4.

Substitutions: When some of the fresh fruits are not available, you might want to use mandarin oranges, pineapple chunks, mango slices or chunks, red grapes, frozen blueberries or blackberries. I don't recommend frozen strawberries or raspberries for this dish as they become "mushy," nor do I recommend bananas, apples or pears, as they discolor quickly.

Autumn

The autumn months offer a bit of a
respite between the rush of summer
vacation and the frenzy of the holidays.
Why not enjoy this interlude by relaxing
over dinner with friends? Celebrate
the culinary bounty of the harvest.

Chicken alla Parma
Lemon Risotto
Zucchini Ribbons
Red Pepper Coulis

Tomato Mousse with Avocado

Grilled Sake Shrimp
Coconut Ginger Sweet Potatoes
Stir-Fried Vegetables

Crab Cakes with Plum "Vinaigrette"
Northwest Salad

Coconut Tart

Apple Cider Glazed Pork Chops
Garlic Mashed Potatoes
Roasted Tomatoes Provençal

Eggplant Fans with Onion Marmalade

Molten Chocolate Cakes

Autumn Menus

IN HONOR OF AUTUMN COLORS

Tomato Mousse with Avocado

Chicken alla Parma

Lemon Risotto

Zucchini Ribbons

Red Pepper Coulis

Apple Cider Ice Cream

PAN-PACIFIC EXOTICA

Hot Melon Skewers

Grilled Sake Shrimp

Coconut Ginger Sweet Potatoes

Stir-Fried Vegetables

Quick Mango Mousse

INTIMATE HARVEST SUPPER

Butternut Squash Soup

Crab Cakes with Plum Vinaigrette

Northwest Salad

Coconut Tart

EXQUISITE AUTUMNAL EQUINOX DINNER

Eggplant Fans with Onion Marmalade

Apple Cider Glazed Pork Chops

Garlic Mashed Potatoes

Roasted Tomatoes Provençal

Molten Chocolate Cakes

In Honor of Autumn Colors

Tomato Mousse
with
Avocado

◆

Chicken alla Parma

Lemon Risotto
or
Garlic Mashed Potatoes

Zucchini Ribbons

Red Pepper Coulis

Light bodied Pinot Noir or
Sauvignon Blanc

◆

Apple Cider Ice Cream

◆

Coffee or Tea

In Honor of Autumn Colors

Three days ahead:
Prepare the base for **Tomato Mousse**. Continue preparation through addition of cream. Cover tightly and chill.
Prepare **Red Pepper Coulis**.
Fold the napkins if desired.

Two days ahead:
Prepare the base for **Apple Cider Ice Cream**; chill.

The day before:
Prepare chicken breasts for baking **Chicken alla Parma**. Cover with foil, refrigerate.
Slice the **Zucchini Ribbons**; wrap and refrigerate.
Put butter on its serving plate or bowl, cover and refrigerate.
Chill the wine and other cold beverages.
Set up coffee or tea tray, after dinner drinks, glasses, etc.
Make ice.
Set the table. Put out any non-food items (salt and pepper, wine coaster, etc.)
Arrange the flowers.

The morning before:
Chop tomato and snip chives for **Tomato Mousse** garnish.
Add Calvados and freeze **Apple Cider Ice Cream**.
Set up coffee maker.

1 – 2 hours before guests arrive:
Prepare vinaigrette for **Tomato Mousse**.
Remove butter from refrigerator to soften.
Slice purchased bread, if serving.

Before your guests arrive:
Preheat the plates and platters as needed.
Preheat the oven for **Chicken alla Parma**, remove chicken from refrigerator.
Slice avocado for **Tomato Mousse** garnish; arrange on plates. Complete plates with **Tomato Mousse**, garnish and set aside in cool place.
If you must, prepare **Lemon Risotto**; cover and keep warm.

After the guests arrive:
If you don't mind having your guests hang around in the kitchen, prepare the **Lemon Risotto** just before serving.
Sauté the **Zucchini Ribbons**.
Rewarm the **Red Pepper Coulis**.
Bake **Chicken alla Parma**. Arrange on serving plates with additional menu items. Serve.

Tomato Mousse

A very small portion of this velvety smooth, melt-in-your-mouth mousse is to be served to tease the palate, in anticipation of delicious things to come.

1 (14.5-ounce) can diced tomatoes with onion
2 teaspoons tomato paste
1 parsley stem (no leaves)
1 small bay leaf
1 sprig fresh thyme, or ¼ teaspoon dried thyme
½ package gelatin
salt and white pepper to taste
¾ cup whipping cream

for garnish:
1 avocado, ripe but firm, thinly sliced
lemon vinaigrette *(see sidebar)*
2 teaspoons freshly snipped chives
2 – 3 teaspoons diced fresh tomato

In 9 or 10-inch skillet over medium-high heat, cook tomatoes, paste and herbs 20 to 30 minutes, reducing to about one cup. Remove the herb stalks. Puree the tomato mixture in a blender or food processor, then strain through a sieve if desired. *The mixture can be prepared to this point three days ahead. Cover and refrigerate, or freeze up to three months. Thaw the mixture and warm to continue.*

In a small bowl sprinkle gelatin over 2 tablespoons water to soften. Let stand 3 to 4 minutes. The mixture will turn into a lump, that's OK. Meanwhile, prepare an ice bath: in a large wide bowl, place about 2 inches of ice, cover with cold water. Set aside.

Tomato mixture should be very warm but not hot to the touch. Add softened gelatin, stir until gelatin melts and there are no visible granules. Heat gently if needed to melt the gelatin. Cool in the ice bath to 65°F. The mixture should become slightly thickened, but not lumpy. If it gets too cold and starts to set up, just warm it up a bit. Slightly over-season the tomato mixture with salt and white pepper.

In a large bowl, whip the cream to soft peaks *(see sidebar p. 62)*. Whisk one-third of the whipped cream into the cooled tomato mixture. Gently pour tomato and cream mixture over the remaining whipped cream. Fold together until no streaks are visible. Correct seasonings. Chill until set, at least one hour. *Can be prepared 2-3 days ahead.*

To serve, arrange avocado slices on serving plates. Drizzle with vinaigrette. Using hot damp spoon, scoop ovals of mousse; place beside avocado slices. Sprinkle with chopped tomato and chives.

Serves 4 to 6.

EXTRA TOUCHES

LEMON VINAIGRETTE

1 tablespoon freshly squeezed
     lemon juice
1/2 teaspoon mustard
salt and pepper to taste
3 tablespoons Extra-virgin olive oil

Combine lemon juice, mustard, salt and pepper; whisk to dissolve salt. Continue whisking constantly, gradually adding oil to create an emulsion. You can prepare the dressing as much as two hours in advance and store at room temperature until use.

Chicken alla Parma

This recipe was inspired by a meal I had at a bed and breakfast called The Burleigh Court Hotel. The hotel, situated in the Cotswolds west of London, with its wonderful dining room is a favorite of mine and my friends. A heady aroma of sage, prosciutto and peppers will be wafting from your kitchen to call everyone to dinner.

4 boneless, skinless chicken breasts, trimmed of fat
    (*about 4 ounces each*)
1 tablespoon olive oil
freshly ground pepper
4 fresh sage leaves
4 very thin slices of Prosciutto
parchment paper

lemon risotto (recipe follows) or
    garlic mashed potatoes (*see recipe on p. 75*)
zucchini ribbons (recipe follows)
red pepper coulis, heated (recipe follows)
fresh sage leaves, for garnish

Pat chicken breasts dry. Rub each with a little of the olive oil and sprinkle with pepper. With the smooth, shiny sides up, place a fresh sage leaf on each breast. Diagonally wrap each breast with a slice of prosciutto, tucking the ends under and placing seam side down on baking sheet lined with parchment paper. Cover with foil. *If preparing in advance, you can hold here, in refrigerator up to 24 hours. Before continuing, allow chicken to come to room temperature, about 20 minutes.*

Bake chicken covered in preheated 475°F oven for 8 minutes. Remove foil; return to oven until prosciutto just begins to brown at edges, about 1 to 2 minutes more. Check for doneness: the internal temperature should be 145°F. The internal temperature will continue to rise even after removing from the heat. Remove chicken from oven. *If the chicken is ready before you are, you can hold the chicken in 160°F oven, tented with foil for about 10 minutes.*

To serve: in center of each of 4 dinner plates, place about ¾ cup risotto or garlic mashed potatoes, spread into 3½ inch circle. Top with one fourth of the zucchini ribbons. Diagonally slice chicken breasts in thirds; place atop zucchini. Surround each with one fourth of the red pepper coulis. Garnish with fresh sage leaves.

Serves 4.

KNOW YOUR INGREDIENTS

Prosciutto is the Italian word for ham (pronounced proh-SHOO-toh). Red to pink in color, its flavor is a bit salty, and ever so slightly sweet. When sliced very thinly, it almost melts in your mouth! It comes from the hindquarter of pork, that has been salt-cured (but not smoked), dried and aged.

The very best prosciutto comes from Parma, Italy, and is sometimes called **Parma ham**. It is of the highest quality, and like a fine wine, it should never be cooked, so it should not be used for this recipe.

COOKING CLASS

RISOTTO

Making great **risotto** is not difficult, but it is demanding, as you must follow the cooking technique closely to obtain a good quality finished product. A good risotto should be creamy, and "pourable," but not soupy, and a little chewy.

There are **four rules of risotto:**

1. Do not add too much liquid at once.

2. You must stir, stir, stir, without stopping.

3. Proper rice is essential. Use Italian short-grain rice, known as Arborio or Tesori*, or American Risotto rice.

4. Risotto is best served immediately upon completion.

Once the basic technique is mastered, the possibilities and combinations are virtually endless.

To the cooked risotto, you may want to add cooked vegetables, meats, chicken, shrimp, etc. to create a great main dish. A very nice combination includes a small jar of marinated artichoke hearts, drained, and ½ pound cooked, shelled and deveined shrimp.

Lemon Risotto

The Italians call it "Risotto all'Limone" — a mouthwatering, creamy, lemony side dish that is true Italian "comfort food." I love it just like this, or as a main course, with seafood and vegetables added. Because it is very best served immediately after preparation it is a fun dish to prepare while chatting with your guests over drinks.

2 cups chicken stock
2 tablespoons butter
¼ cup finely chopped onion
½ teaspoon salt
1 cup Arborio rice*
½ cup dry white wine
freshly grated zest of one lemon
1 tablespoon freshly squeezed lemon juice
freshly ground pepper, to taste
¼ cup freshly grated Parmesan

In small saucepan, heat chicken stock just to simmer; cover and keep hot.

In medium saucepan over medium-high heat, melt butter. Add onion and salt, sauté just until onion is translucent, about 3 minutes. While stirring, add rice, pouring it in "like rain," so that each grain is separate. Continue sautéing and stirring about 4 minutes more. Rice will become slightly more opaque.

Add wine, lemon zest and juice, stirring. As you stir, drag the spoon across the bottom of the pan; when you can see the dry pan at the bottom as you drag the spoon across, add about ¼ cup of the hot chicken stock. It is important not to let the rice dry out at this point. Continue cooking and stirring. Each time you see the dry pan add about ¼ cup of stock until all of the stock has been added. This will take about 20 minutes. Taste for doneness. The risotto should be slightly chewy in the center, or "al dente" as the Italians call it. Stir in the Parmesan cheese. Correct the seasonings if necessary. Serve immediately if at all possible. If you must prepare this dish a few minutes in advance, keep warm, and stir in about 3 tablespoons of stock to restore the consistency before serving.

Makes 4 side dish servings.

Arborio and Tesori rices are imported from Italy and found in Italian deli markets or large supermarkets. You may also use American risotto rice, available in some supermarkets. All have the fat, roundish grain, which will absorb a large quantity of liquid without becoming mushy.

Zucchini Ribbons

The locals of Whidbey Island, Washington all say that the biggest problem they face in zucchini season is that you MUST lock your car. Otherwise, you may return to find the backseat filled with zucchini! That memory always makes me smile when I make this dish. The zucchini, pale green and shiny, tender and fresh tasting, zucchini is a perfect accompaniment for the flavors of Chicken alla Parma.

3 medium zucchini, washed, ends trimmed (*about ½ pound*)
2 teaspoons olive oil
salt and pepper, to taste

Half each zucchini lengthwise, remove seeds if desired. With flat side of vegetable down on cutting board, thinly slice the zucchini lengthwise into ribbons about 1/16 inch thick, and no more than 1 inch wide. *You may prepare up to this point in advance: wrap the ribbons in plastic and refrigerate overnight.*

Heat olive oil in large skillet over medium high heat. Add zucchini and about ½ teaspoon salt. Sauté, stirring, just until zucchini become soft and pliable. Take care not to overcook. Remove from heat and correct the seasonings. Serve immediately.

Serves 4.

Note: To make a very fast, light vegetarian entrée, prepare zucchini as directed here, then top with the red pepper sauce, or the red pepper and tomato sauce variation, both on the next page. A very colorful and delicious, low fat alternative to pasta.

KNOW YOUR INGREDIENTS

OLIVE OIL

Olive oil ranges in color from golden yellow to deep green, depending on the varieties of olives pressed. I have found that the "greener" the oil, the stronger the taste and aroma. French olive oils tend to be lighter in taste; Greek oils tend to be "peppery" tasting. Italian and Spanish olive oils tend to be more "olivey." Do try several different brands of oil to find the one or two you like best.

Storage conditions can affect the quality of the oil. Store your olive oil in a cool dry place, as heat and light destroy the oil's flavor. It does not need refrigeration. Don't buy more that you can use within six to eight months, as with any fat, it will go rancid.

Olive oil grades are determined by the amount of oleic acid in the oil set by Italian law. EXTRA-VIRGIN olive oil contains the least amount of oleic acid; PURE olive oil contains more. PURE olive oil is not a lesser quality oil, but it is typically less expensive. It is a good choice for sautéing foods.

EXTRA-VIRGIN and VIRGIN olive oils come from the first pressing of the olives, usually a cold pressing. These are the most expensive of the olive oils, and are packaged in smaller quantities. They tend to be less "oily," having a lighter, finer taste on the palate. For this reason in any dish served at room temperature, or if olive oil is an integral part of the dish, you should use EXTRA-VIRGIN OIL.

TECHNIQUE

ROASTING PEPPERS

Roasting peppers is an easy task, but can be time consuming. However, it is a task that can be accomplished 1 or 2 days in advance.

First, line a baking sheet with foil. Split peppers in half lengthwise; remove seeds and ribs. Rinse if necessary, and dry thoroughly.

Lay pepper halves cut side down on foil; bake at 450°F until skins are charred black, about 7 to 10 minutes.

Remove from oven; wrap peppers in the foil from the baking sheet, seal. This will steam the peppers, making the skins easy to remove.

When peppers are cool enough to handle, rub black skin away with paper towels.

If you are preparing peppers in advance, seal in an airtight container and refrigerate up to 2 days.

This roasting technique applies to all varieties of peppers: bell, jalapeno, Anaheim, serrano, or other types.

If you are working with hot chilies, be sure to wear rubber gloves to protect your hands, and take special care not to touch your face. The hot chilies can cause chemical burns.

Red Pepper Coulis

A coulis is defined as a smooth, uncooked or lightly cooked, very fresh tasting sauce. With its rich, fresh flavor, this sauce is the crowning touch to Chicken alla Parma.

3 large, ripe red bell peppers, roasted and peeled (*about 1 pound*) or
    1 (15-ounce) jar of roasted peppers, drained
1 to 2 tablespoons chicken stock (optional)
salt, to taste
red hot pepper sauce, to taste

Puree one-third of the roasted peppers in a food processor or blender. Add remaining peppers, pulse process to a chunky consistency. Add chicken stock to thin sauce, if necessary. Season to taste with salt and hot pepper sauce. *The coulis may be prepared in advance and refrigerated up to one week, or frozen for up to six months.*

Makes about 1 cup sauce.

Note: This is a very versatile and flavorful sauce to serve with fish or meats. Or combine with 2 cups tomato sauce, heat through and serve on pasta!

Apple Cider Ice Cream

Each fall my family makes the trek over the mountains to Eastern Washington. The autumn foliage is always spectacular. We take advantage to taste the many varieties and to stock up on the season's best apples. My favorite apple vendor produces outstanding cider, which is the basis for this recipe. It is the essence of autumn's bounty, captured by succulent, sweet apple cider married with extravagant cream.

4 egg yolks
1 cup heavy cream
1 cup milk
¾ cup apple cider, or dry sparkling cider
½ cup sugar
1 large cinnamon stick
1½ tablespoons Calvados apple brandy (optional)

purchased caramel sauce, for garnish
hazelnuts
fresh mint sprigs

Whisk the egg yolks lightly in a large bowl and set aside. In a large heavy saucepan over medium heat, bring the cream and milk to a boil; remove from heat.

Combine the apple cider, sugar, and cinnamon sticks in a non-reactive saucepan *(see sidebar)*. Cook over high heat until the mixture reduces and turns a dark amber color, 20 to 25 minutes. Remove the cinnamon sticks and immediately whisk the mixture into the warm cream and milk, incorporating about a third at a time. Be careful — the cream will spatter and bubble up. But the caramelized cider MUST be poured into the cream as quickly as possible or it will continue to cook and burn the pan. When all the caramel has been whisked in, reheat the cream, stirring constantly, until the cider is completely incorporated.

Pour a quarter of the hot mixture into the egg yolks, whisking continuously, then pour it back into the saucepan and cook over low heat, stirring constantly with a wooden spoon until the mixture thickens enough to coat the back of the spoon. Strain the custard through a fine mesh strainer into a bowl. Whisk it a few times to release the heat, then refrigerate the custard until thoroughly chilled. *This can be accomplished 24 to 48 hours in advance.*

When completely chilled, stir in the Calvados. Freeze the custard in an ice cream freezer according to the manufacturer's directions.

Serve ice cream topped with caramel sauce, hazelnuts and mint sprigs.

Makes 1 quart.

THE RIGHT TOOLS

A **non-reactive pan** is one that will not react with the acids in foods. Therefore, it must be made of stainless steel, tin, or glass, or lined with non-stick, enamel or porcelain. Do not use cast iron or aluminum when cooking acidic foods, such as tomatoes, fruit juices, wine or vinegar, as the metal pan can react with these types of foods, lending a metallic flavor or a grayish color.

Pan-Pacific Exotica

Hot Melon Skewers

◆

Grilled Sake Shrimp

Coconut Ginger Sweet Potatoes

Stir-Fried Vegetables

Chardonnay

◆

Quick Mango Mousse

◆

Coffee or Tea

Pan-Pacific Exotica

Three days ahead:
Prepare the mango puree for the **Quick Mango Mousse.**
Fold the napkins if desired.

Two days ahead:
Prepare marinade for **Grilled Sake Shrimp.**
Rewarm the fruit puree to dissolve sugar, then cool slightly and add gelatin. Finish preparation of **Quick Mango Mousse.**
Divide mousse into individual serving dishes, cover and chill.

The day before:
Cut vegetables for **Stir-Fried Vegetables.**
Put butter on its serving plate or bowl, cover and refrigerate.
Chill the wine and other cold beverages.
Set up coffee or tea tray, after dinner drinks, glasses, etc.
Make ice.
Set the table. Put out any non-food items (salt and pepper, wine coaster, etc.)
Arrange the flowers.

The morning before:
Wash mint sprigs for **Quick Mango Mousse** garnish. Chill.
Set up coffee maker.

6 hours before guests arrive:
Soak skewers for **Grilled Sake Shrimp.** Clean, peel and devein shrimp if necessary. Skewer shrimp. Marinate ½ hour.
Remove from marinade, pat dry, refrigerate.

1 – 2 hours before guests arrive:
Prepare marinade and melon pieces for **Hot Melon Skewers.** Mix and refrigerate.
Prepare **Coconut Ginger Sweet Potatoes.** Tent with foil; keep warm in 160° oven.
Whip cream for garnish for **Quick Mango Mousse.** Chill.
Remove butter from refrigerator to soften.
Slice purchased bread, if serving.

Before your guests arrive:
Skewer **Hot Melon** pieces; arrange on serving tray.
Preheat the grill or broiler for **Grilled Sake Shrimp.**
Preheat the plates and platters as needed.

After the guests arrive:
Stir-fry the **Vegetables.**
Grill or broil the **Grilled Sake Shrimp.** Serve on warmed plates with accompaniments.

CHILI PASTE

*A little Asian chili paste adds heat
and zip to your recipes. It is a
combination of ground chilis, salt and
vinegar usually with either onion or
garlic added. Use some restraint,
these chili pastes pack quite a punch.
You can find them in larger supermarkets with the Asian foods, or at
Asian specialty shops.*

Hot Melon Skewers

*A mouthwatering twist on the usual melon ball —
with a bit of heat and zip, yet refreshing and light.
These also make a lovely accompaniment to a
sophisticated brunch menu.*

½ cup rice vinegar
2 tablespoons superfine sugar
⅛ teaspoon salt
½ teaspoon chili paste *(see sidebar at left)*
2-3 cups assorted melons, cut into 1-inch cubes or balls
short wooden skewers or cocktail picks

In large bowl, dissolve sugar and salt in vinegar, add chili paste.
Pour mixture over melon pieces; stir gently to coat. Let stand at
least 15 minutes, or as long as 2 hours. Skewer 3 or four melon
pieces on each wooden pick or skewer. Chill if desired.

Makes 16 to 20 appetizers.

Grilled Sake Shrimp

Fusion food is very popular on the West Coast. This dish, inspired by Chef Steve Black of San Diego, takes bits of Thai and Japanese cuisine, melding them together for an exotic dinner.

for marinade (makes about ¾ cup marinade):
2 cloves garlic, peeled
1 shallot
1 teaspoon fresh ginger, minced
1 teaspoon pickled ginger (optional)
2 tablespoons black bean paste or sauce (optional)
1 teaspoon hot pepper sauce (optional)
1½ teaspoon honey
2 tablespoons Sweet Thai chili sauce
2 tablespoons Dry sake
1 tablespoon soy sauce
¼ cup olive oil

8 bamboo skewers
16 very large shrimp, peeled and deveined, tails left on
  (see sidebar on p. 24)
  (under 10 count, about 1¾ pounds)

Blend all ingredients for marinade in blender until smooth. *This can be done 1 or 2 days ahead. Refrigerate to store.*

Soak skewers in water for an hour, drain. With two skewers held parallel about ¾ inch apart, skewer 4 shrimp. This prevents shrimp from rotating on the skewers. Pour marinade into a shallow non-reactive pan. Place shrimp skewers in pan, turn to coat. Let marinate no more than one half hour, preferably at room temperature, turning at least once. Remove from marinade. *Prepare up to four hours ahead to this point. Cover and refrigerate shrimp. Allow to stand 15 minutes at room temperature before cooking.*

Meanwhile, preheat grill. Brush preheated grill with oil. GRILL MUST BE VERY HOT, or honey will make the shrimp stick. Pat shrimp dry with paper towels. Grill shrimp just until opaque, turning once or twice.

To serve, slide shrimp off skewers. Mound Coconut Ginger Sweet Potatoes in center of serving plate; surround with wreath of Stir-Fried Vegetables. Place shrimp atop vegetables. Serve immediately.

Serves 4.

Variation:
Prepare marinade as directed. With very sharp knife, cut 4 boneless, skinless chicken breasts into thin strips. Marinate chicken strips on skewers. Grill as directed above.

KNOW YOUR INGREDIENTS

GINGER

Ginger is a tropical root characterized by its peppery sweet, spicy fragrance and flavor. **Fresh ginger** *should be firm with a light tan, smooth skin and a fresh spicy aroma. Use it peeled, then grate or sliver it. Fresh ginger will keep refrigerated, tightly wrapped; or peeled in a jar, covered with sherry for up to two weeks. The resulting ginger flavored sherry can be used for cooking as well. Ginger may be frozen for up to two months. To use, just slice off the amount you need from the unthawed root, return the remainder to the freezer. Fresh ginger can be found in large supermarkets or Asian markets.*

Pickled ginger *has been preserved in sweet vinegar.*

BLACK BEAN PASTE

Black bean paste *is made from fermented small black soybeans and is extremely salty. It is used to flavor Asian dishes.*

SWEET THAI CHILI SAUCE

Sweet Thai chili sauce *is a sweetened blend of red chilies, garlic and vinegar. Although it is not as fiery as hot Thai chili sauce it still packs a punch.*

Pickled ginger, black bean paste and sweet Thai chili sauce are available in the Asian section of your supermarket or at Asian grocers.

DRY SAKE

Dry Sake *is Japanese rice wine. Slightly sweet, this wine amplifies the flavors of the marinade.*

SWEET POTATOES VS. YAMS

Although they may look similar, yams and sweet potatoes come from two different plants. Sweet potatoes are most common in the U.S. Yams are not widely grown or sold here, coming from South America, Asia and Africa. But in the United States south-erners often call sweet potatoes "yams." The confusion is heightened by the fact that canned sweet potatoes are quite often labeled "yams."

There are two varieties of sweet potatoes. The first, pale skinned with pale yellow flesh is not sweet after cooking and has a flavor resembling that of a baking potato. The other has dark orange skin and vivid orange sweet flesh. It cooks to a much lighter, sweeter consistency. I recommend the second variety for this dish.

The varieties of yams are too numerous to mention here. Chances are, the one you find in the store is a sweet potato.

Look for medium-size sweet potatoes with smooth unbruised skin. Sweet potatoes lose flavor when refrigerated before cooking. Do not store them for long periods of time, so buy only what you can use within a week. Sweet potatoes are a good source of iron, calcium and vitamins A and C.

COCONUT MILK

Coconut milk and coconut cream are both preparations of water and fresh coconut, coconut cream having a much higher percentage of coconut to water than coconut milk. Coconut cream is richer and tastes more like coconut than the milk. You can find canned coconut cream in large super-markets and Asian specialty markets. Do not confuse it with Cream of Coconut, which is sweetened.

Coconut Ginger Sweet Potatoes

No one in my family likes yams or sweet potatoes, including myself. But we really enjoy this particular side dish with its unique flavors. Who would have known?

1 – 2 sweet potatoes (*about 1 pound*)
½ teaspoon salt
½ – ¾ cup coconut milk
2 teaspoons butter
1 tablespoon brown sugar
½ teaspoon ground ginger
salt and white pepper to taste

Wash, peel and cut sweet potatoes into evenly sized chunks. Barely cover sweet potatoes with cold water, cover and bring to boil. Add salt to water and remove lid from pan. Cook until sweet potatoes are fork tender; drain well. Mash with remaining ingredients. *You can prepare this dish up to two hours ahead: place prepared sweet potatoes in an ovenproof bowl and tent with foil. Hold in a 160°F oven. Stir to restore consistency before serving.* Serve piping hot.

Makes four servings.

Stir-Fried Vegetables

1 – 2 tablespoons sesame oil
2 leeks, white and light green part only, cut in julienne strips
1 carrot, peeled and cut in julienne strips
½ each red and yellow bell pepper, cut in julienne strips
2 ribs celery, sliced on the diagonal, ¼ inch thick
⅛ teaspoon salt
6 mushrooms, sliced
2 cloves garlic, minced
1 – 2 teaspoons freshly grated ginger
2 tablespoons oyster sauce
water
1 small head bok choy, cut in julienne strips
soy sauce

Over high heat, heat sesame oil in large sauté pan or wok. Add leeks, carrot, peppers and celery with salt. Cook until vegetables begin to soften. Add mushrooms, garlic and ginger, cook two minutes more. Moisten with oyster sauce and water if necessary. Add bok choy, toss and heat through. Season with soy sauce. Serve immediately.

Serves 4.

Leeks, carrot, bell peppers, celery and mushrooms may be cut one day in advance. Store in airtight containers in refrigerator until ready to use.

TECHNIQUES

LEEKS

To clean leeks, first trim away the root end. Then make a lengthwise slice from the dark green part of the leek through the white portion, exposing all of the layers but leaving the leaves intact at the green end. Separate the layers and wash under cold running water to rid any accumulated sand. Then cut off the dark green portion. Placing the cut side of the leek down, slice the layers into julienne strips.

KNOW YOUR INGREDIENTS

OYSTER SAUCE

Oyster sauce is a popular, widely available Oriental seasoning. It is a thick concentrated sauce made with oysters, brine and soy sauce. The sauce is an essential flavor element brightening the flavor of the vegetables in your stir-fry dishes and adding richness. Look for the bottles in the Asian section of your supermarket or at an Asian grocer.

BOK CHOY

Also known as Chinese white cabbage, bok choy has thick white stalks and dark green leaves with white veins. It adds crunch to your stir-fry. Look for bright white stalks and glossy green leaves without brown spots. Store in a plastic bag in the refrigerator. Use within a day or two.

Quick Mango Mousse

This sophisticated velvety smooth dessert will be a show-stopper after dinner. No one will believe how easily it is prepared — so, don't tell them!

1 package gelatin
1 cup mango puree *(see fruit purees in Show-Offs!!)*
2 – 4 tablespoons sugar
1 cup heavy cream
1 tablespoon orange or coconut liqueur (optional)

for garnish:
fresh fruit, whipped cream, mint sprigs

In a small bowl sprinkle gelatin over 2 tablespoons water to soften. Let stand 3 to 4 minutes. The mixture will turn into a lump, that's OK. Meanwhile, prepare an ice bath: in a large wide bowl, place about 2 inches of ice, cover with cold water. Set aside.

In small saucepan, combine mango puree and sugar. The amount of sugar will need to be adjusted for the sweetness already in the fruit. Sweeten to taste; then add a little more sugar because the mixture will taste less sweet as is chills. Heat the fruit and sugar over low heat until the sugar dissolves. Remove from the heat. The temperature of the fruit mixture will need to be lower than 160°F for the next step, or the gelatin will be ruined.

In a large bowl, whip the cream to soft peaks *(see sidebar)*. Refrigerate until ready to use.

When gelatin is softened, stir it into the warm mango mixture. Very carefully heat if necessary to melt the gelatin. When gelatin granules are no longer visible, remove from the heat. Cool in the ice bath to 65°F. The mixture should become slightly thickened, but not lumpy. If it gets too cold and starts to set up, just warm it up a bit. Add liqueur.

Whisk one-third of the whipped cream into the cooled mango mixture. Gently pour fruit and cream mixture over the remaining whipped cream. Fold together until no streaks are visible. Immediately spoon into 4 serving bowls, ramekins or stemmed glasses. Chill until set, at least one hour. *If preparing further in advance, cover tightly with plastic wrap.*

Serve garnished with fresh fruit, a dollop of whipped cream and a mint sprig.

Serves 4.

Variations on this recipe are nearly endless, just substitute different fruit puree sand liqueurs for different flavors. See the Fruit Purees recipe for directions.

COOKING CLASS

WHIPPING CREAM OR EGG WHITES

When a recipe calls for whipped cream or beaten egg whites, it is essential to know how stiff the egg whites or cream should be. Periodically stop the whisking, lift the whisk from the bowl and look at the peak that is formed.

Soft peaks *are characterized by a swirled, loop shaped peak similar to those famous ice cream cones.*

Medium peaks *bend to the side, but not all the way over.*

And ***stiff peaks*** *are just that, they stand straight in the air.*

Be patient, keep checking those peaks. Your recipe will be more successful if you obtain the right texture.

Intimate Harvest Supper

Butternut Squash Soup

◆

Crab Cakes
With
Plum Vinaigrette

Northwest Salad

Sourdough Bread
(purchased)

Reisling
(served very cold)
or
Pinot Noir

◆

Coconut Tart

◆

Coffee or Tea

Intimate Harvest Supper

Three days ahead:
Fold the napkins if desired.
Peel and chop onion and squash for **Butternut Squash Soup**. Wrap and chill.
Chop nuts for **Butternut Squash Soup**.
Prepare **Caramelized Nuts** for **Northwest Salad**.

Two days ahead:
Prepare **Butternut Squash Soup**. Chill.
Prepare, chill and blind bake pastry for **Coconut Tart**. Cover and set aside.

The day before:
Shop for fruit garnish for **Coconut Tart**.
Prepare **Coconut Tart** filling. Bake, cover and set aside.
Combine ingredients for **Crab Cakes** and shape into patties, roll in breadcrumbs.
Prepare dressing for **Northwest Salad**.
Put butter on its serving plate or bowl, cover and refrigerate.
Chill the wine and other cold beverages.
Set up coffee or tea tray, after dinner drinks, glasses, etc.
Make ice.
Set the table. Put out any non-food items (salt and pepper, wine coaster, etc.)
Arrange the flowers.

The morning before:
Prepare plum sauce for **Crab Cakes with Plum "Vinaigrette."** Set aside.
Wash and prepare fresh fruit for garnish for **Coconut Tart**.
Wash and dry greens for **Northwest Salad**. Chill.
Set up coffee maker.

1 – 2 hours before guests arrive:
Remove butter from refrigerator to soften.
Slice purchased bread, if serving.
Slice **Coconut Tart** into wedges, plate, garnish and set aside until serving time.

Before your guests arrive:
Reheat **Butternut Squash Soup**. Stir in Calvados. Slice apple garnish.
Preheat the plates and platters as needed.

After the guests arrive:
Garnish and serve **Butternut Squash Soup**.
Toss greens and dressing, finish preparation for **Northwest Salad**.
Sauté **Crab Cakes**, garnish and serve on warmed plates.

SWEATING VEGETABLES

Many soup and sauce recipes begin with cooking aromatic vegetables to soften their textures and to concentrate the flavor. A small amount of salt is necessary to draw the moisture out of the food. During the cooking process you will notice some moisture being released from the vegetables, hence the term "sweating." Continue cooking until the moisture has evaporated.

Cooking the vegetables slowly over medium-low or medium heat will accomplish this goal without risk of browning or burning. If the vegetables begin to cook too quickly, simply remove them from the heat for a few seconds to cool, and lower the heat.

THE RIGHT TOOLS

SEIVES

Passing soups and sauces through a sieve creates a very smooth, fine textured result. The finer the sieve, the smoother the result. Most kitchens have a coarse mesh sieve of some kind. You may want to invest in a fine mesh sieve for velvety smooth sauces and soups.

Butternut Squash Soup

Comfort food on a cold autumn evening. And yet, the velvety texture of this soup screams elegance. Topped with thinly sliced apple and nut oil the presentation is art in a bowl.

2 tablespoons butter
1 medium onion, coarsely chopped
½ teaspoon thyme
½ teaspoon curry powder
2 tablespoons flour
1 cup best quality chicken stock
1 cup apple juice
½ pound butternut squash, peeled, seeded and cut in 1-inch pieces
½ cup heavy cream or evaporated milk
salt and white pepper, to taste
1 tablespoon Calvados (apple Brandy)

for garnish:
8 very thin wedges of Granny Smith apple
1 tablespoon hazelnut or walnut oil*
1 tablespoon finely chopped hazelnuts or walnuts*
Use the same variety of oil as nut

In large saucepan, melt butter over medium heat. Add onion and a pinch of salt. Cook until onion is translucent but not brown. Add thyme and curry powder, cook 1 minute longer. Sprinkle flour over onion mixture, whisk until smooth. Cook 3 to 4 minutes. Slowly add stock and apple juice, then the squash. Raise the heat to high and bring to a boil. Cook until squash is VERY tender, 20 to 30 minutes. Remove from the heat. Allow to cool briefly.

Transfer the mixture to a blender in small batches, taking care to fill blender jar no more than half full. Personal experience has taught me that hot liquids tend to "blow up" in the blender if it is filled too full or started at high speed. Hold the lid on the blender jar tightly with a potholder or kitchen towel, THEN turn on blender, starting at low speed. Increase speed to puree the soup until smooth. Strain soup through a sieve if desired.**

Return to heat. Add cream and correct the seasonings. *The soup can be made 2 days ahead to this point and refrigerated, or frozen for 4 months.*

Just before serving whisk in Calvados. To serve, ladle into bowls, insert apple slices, drizzle with nut oil and sprinkle with ground nuts.

Makes about four cups soup.

Flavored oils can be found in larger supermarkets and specialty stores. They keep well for about a year in a cool, dark cupboard.

Crab Cakes with Plum "Vinaigrette"

Dungeness Bay is just north of the Olympic Peninsula in Washington; crab is plentiful here. This dish is a bit of fusion of Northwest and Pacific Rim.

1 cup fine dry white bread crumbs
½ teaspoon Old Bay seasoning, divided
½ pound crab meat, Dungeness if you can get it
3 tablespoons red bell pepper, finely diced
3 tablespoons yellow bell pepper, finely diced
½ small onion, finely minced
1 tablespoon freshly minced parsley
1 teaspoon freshly squeezed lemon juice
dash of Tabasco sauce
¼ cup Mayonnaise
¼ teaspoon salt

for vinaigrette:
½ cup plum sauce*
1 tablespoon rice vinegar
dash of Tabasco sauce

2 tablespoons butter

2 scallions, thinly sliced on the diagonal

Combine breadcrumbs and ¼ teaspoon Old Bay seasoning in a wide shallow bowl. Set aside.

Flake crab into a large bowl. Measure 1 tablespoon each of the diced bell peppers, set aside. Add the remaining peppers to the crab with the onion, parsley, lemon juice, Tabasco sauce, Mayonnaise, salt and the remaining ¼ teaspoon Old Bay seasoning; stir to combine.

Divide crab mixture into 4 equal portions. If desired, divide each portion in half again, to make petite crab cakes. Roll each portion into a ball. Roll balls in the seasoned breadcrumbs, and then flatten into ½-inch thick disks. Chill well. *The crab cakes can be made one day ahead and refrigerated, or frozen up to two months.*

For the "vinaigrette," stir together the plum sauce, rice vinegar and Tabasco sauce. Set aside.

Just before serving, in a large skillet over medium heat melt the butter until it sizzles. Gently add crab cakes. Sauté until golden on both sides, 3 to 4 minutes per side. Serve hot in a puddle of plum "vinaigrette." Sprinkle with the reserved red and yellow peppers and scallions.

Serves 4.

Plum sauce is found in the Asian or Oriental section of your supermarket and at Asian markets.

COOKING CLASS

BREADCRUMBS

Freshly made breadcrumbs are preferable to those in a can. You can utilize those bits of bread leftover from dinner — turn them into breadcrumbs, and store them in a resealable plastic bag in your freezer. Take out what you need.

To make breadcrumbs, cut the crusts off the bread. If the bread is very fresh, you may need to let it dry on a rack for an hour or two. For dry bread crumbs, allow the bread to dry longer. Tear the bread into pieces, place in food processor. Process the bread until crumbs form.

One slice of regular sandwich bread makes about ½ cup breadcrumbs.

USING REMOVABLE BOTTOM TART PANS

A removable bottom or false bottom tart pan is a great addition to your kitchen. Look for a heavyweight pan, the darker the metal the better. There are a few tricks associated with great results every time.

Lightly spray the bottom and sides of the pan with cooking oil, then wipe out. This will prevent any sticking to the sides of the pan.

Place the pan on a larger one, a pizza pan works well. This will prevent you from picking up the pan and inevitably placing it on your other palm, only to have the bottom fall out!

After lining the pan with pastry, cut off a bit of the excess to make a ball about the size of a walnut. Roll the ball in flour. Use the ball to press the pastry crust into the corners of the tart pan, easing the extra dough to the outside edge.

Rest your rolling pin across the pan at the center. Roll in either direction to instantly cut the pastry even with the edge of the pan. Make sure no pastry hangs over the edge, as it will stick and prevent the bottom from coming loose later on.

Then, go around the top of the pastry crust using your thumb to press the top edge of the pastry against the pan.

Chill, line with a paper cartouche described in the sidebar at right and bake as directed.

When your tart is ready to serve, check to see that the sides of the pastry are not stuck to the pan. Then, rest the bottom of the pan on a small bowl or can. The sides should easily drop away.

Coconut Tart

A rich dark chocolate pastry crust filled with luscious coconut. The surprise raspberry filling layer provides a balance of sweet and tart.

For pastry (makes enough for two 8" tarts):
1 cup flour
⅓ cup cocoa powder
pinch of salt
9 tablespoons butter, softened
3 tablespoons sugar
1 egg, beaten

Sift together flour, cocoa powder and salt. Set aside. Using a mixer or by hand cream butter and sugar until light and fluffy, about 3 minutes. Add flour mixture, stir until combined. Add half of egg, stir until it is incorporated into chocolate mixture. Then add remaining half; stir until incorporated. Divide mixture into two equal portions. Roll each portion into a ball, flatten into a disk. Wrap tightly and refrigerate at least 30 minutes or overnight. *The pastry can be frozen at this point up to two months. Thaw in refrigerator before use.*

Allow pastry disk to stand at room temperature for 5 minutes before working. On lightly floured surface knead one disk to soften slightly. Dough will be sticky. Roll between two sheets of waxed paper or plastic wrap to a diameter of 10 inches, about ⅛ inch thickness. Remove top sheet of wrap. Using bottom sheet, invert into 8-inch removable bottom tart pan. Peel away wrap. Gently press pastry into corners and up sides of pan. Trim top edge with rolling pin. Place pastry pan on a larger tray or pan. Chill 30 minutes.

Preheat oven to 375°F. Line pastry shell with parchment "cartouche" *(see sidebar)*. Fill with pie weights or dried beans. Press weights or beans out to edge of pastry to hold sides up. Bake until top edge of pastry begins to darken, about 10 minutes. Remove pie weights. Return pastry to oven; bake 4 to 5 minutes more, until bottom is dry. Cool on a rack. *The pastry can be baked one day in advance. Cover with a cake cover or an inverted bowl.*

For filling (for two tarts):
6 tablespoons seedless raspberry jam
14 ounces shredded coconut
1 (14-ounce) can sweetened condensed milk
1 teaspoon vanilla or coconut extract

Spread 3 tablespoons jam evenly over bottom of each baked pastry shell. Stir together coconut, sweetened condensed milk and extract. Spread evenly over jam. Bake at 350°F for 22 minutes. Remove from oven and cool on rack. *The tart can be assembled one day in advance. Store in an airtight container. It may also be frozen up to 6 months.*

Cut into wedges to serve garnished with fresh strawberry fans or raspberries.

Serves 8.

COOKING CLASS

MAKING A PAPER "CARTOUCHE"

A "cartouche" is simply a parchment paper circle used to line a pastry crust or top a poaching liquid like a lid. Instead of tracing a circle, try this:

*To make a parchment paper **cartouche**, cut a square about 10 inches. Fold in quarters to a square shape.*

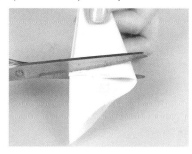

Then fold again pressing folded edges together to form a triangle. Repeat.

Trim the short edge about 5 inches from the center point, and unfold into a circle.

EXTRA TOUCHES

CARAMELIZED NUTS

Caramelized nuts add a wonderful sweet crunch to salads and desserts and are so easy to make:

1/2 cup shelled nuts
   (hazelnuts, pecans, walnuts,
   peanuts)
3-4 tablespoons sugar
dash cayenne pepper (optional)
dash salt (optional)

Heat nuts and sugar in small skillet over high heat. Stir and cook until sugar melts and coats the nuts. Continue to cook until sugar and nuts begin to turn golden. Remove from heat, pour nuts onto sheet pan to cool.

The nuts may be prepared a week ahead and stored in an airtight container.

Northwest Salad

The fanfare of Northwest grapes, nuts, cheese and fresh greens, adorned with the tart-sweet raspberry and basil vinaigrette.

For dressing:
2 tablespoons raspberry vinegar or red wine vinegar
1/4 teaspoon salt
1/4 teaspoon Dijon mustard
2 fresh basil leaves, cut in very fine chiffonade *(see sidebar on p. 39),*
   or 1/2 teaspoon dried basil
6 tablespoons hazelnut or olive oil

4 cups mixed leafy salad greens, washed and dried
1/2 cup seedless red grapes, washed and dried
3 ounces Gorgonzola cheese, crumbled
1/4 cup caramelized hazelnuts or pecans *(see sidebar)*
freshly ground black pepper

For the dressing: in small mixing bowl or blender container, combine vinegar, salt, mustard and basil until salt has dissolved. Starting with a few drops at a time, slowly add the oil, whisking or blending constantly. When one or two tablespoons of the oil have been incorporated into the mixture, you may add the oil slowly in a steady stream. Continue whisking or blending. The vinaigrette should thicken slightly as the last of the oil is added. *To prepare ahead, cover and store at room temperature up to 24 hours in advance. Whisk before using.*

Makes about 1/2 cup dressing.

Place salad greens in large bowl, toss with about 6 tablespoons of the dressing. Arrange greens on individual serving plates if desired. Slice grapes into halves; arrange over greens. Drizzle with remaining 2 tablespoons dressing. Sprinkle with Gorgonzola, candied nuts and freshly ground pepper if desired.

Exquisite Autumnal Equinox Dinner

Eggplant Fans
With
Onion Marmalade

Sauvignon Blanc

◆

Apple Cider Glazed Pork Chops

Garlic Mashed Potatoes

Roasted Tomatoes Provençal

Assorted Breads
(purchased)
And
Flavored Butter
(optional, see recipes in
Show-Offs!! section)

Johannesburg Riesling
(served very cold)
or Merlot

◆

Molten Chocolate Cakes

◆

Coffee or Tea

Exquisite Autumnal Equinox Dinner

Three days ahead:
Slice onions for **Eggplant Fans with Onion Marmalade.** Prepare marmalade, cover and refrigerate.
Prepare fruit coulis for **Molten Chocolate Cakes**, put in "squeezer" container. Cover and refrigerate.
Prepare flavored butters, if desired. Cover and refrigerate.
Fold the napkins if desired.

Two days ahead:
Mince the fresh parsley (it must be DRY) for the **Garlic Mashed Potatoes.** Cover and refrigerate.

The day before:
Prepare the brine mixture for the **Apple Cider Glazed Pork Chops**; store in resealable plastic bag in refrigerator.
Trim the pork chops, cover and refrigerate.
Prepare the **Apple Cider Glaze** for the pork chops, cover and refrigerate.
Put the flavored butter on its serving plate or bowl, cover and refrigerate.
Chill the wine and other cold beverages.
Set up coffee or tea tray, after dinner drinks, glasses, etc.
Make ice.
Set the table. Put out any non-food items (salt and pepper, wine coaster, etc.)
Arrange the flowers.

The morning before:
Cut and stuff **Tomatoes Provençal**; cover and refrigerate.
Prepare batter for **Molten Chocolate Cakes**. Spoon into ramekins; cover and refrigerate.
Wash and prepare berries for garnish and mint garnish for cakes, if desired. Cover and refrigerate.
Whip cream for cakes; refrigerate.
Set up coffee maker.

1 – 2 hours before guests arrive:
Place pork chops in brine for 1 hour.
Peel, cut and cook potatoes for **Garlic Mashed Potatoes**. Complete recipe; place in 160°F holding oven until serving time.
Fan cut eggplants for **Eggplant Fans with Onion Marmalade** and brush with oil. Set aside.
Prepare plates with coulis for the **Molten Chocolate Cakes**.
Remove pork chops from brine after 1 hour, dry chops and set aside to come to room temperature before cooking.
Remove the tomatoes from the refrigerator to come to room temperature before cooking.
Remove butter from refrigerator to soften.
Slice purchased bread, if serving.

Before your guests arrive:
Warm onion marmalade.
Grill eggplants; place on serving plates, complete presentation with onion marmalade, cheese, etc.
Preheat oven and shallow baking pan for pork chops.
Preheat the plates and platters as needed.

After the guests arrive:
Remove **Molten Chocolate Cakes** from refrigerator, let stand at room temperature before baking.
Warm the **Apple Cider Glaze.** Sauté the pork chops, complete the recipe.
Roast the tomatoes.
Whisk the potatoes.
Plate the entrée.
After dinner: Bake the **Molten Chocolate Cakes**, serve.

TECHNIQUE

FAN CUTTING EGGPLANTS

A beautiful, easy presentation for this dish is to cut the eggplants into **fans**.

With a sharp knife, cut thin slices from just below the stem of the eggplant all the way to the bottom, taking care not to separate the slices at the top.

With the heel of your hand, press firmly on the stem end of the eggplant to 'fan out' the slices, making the eggplant lie flat.

This is also a great technique for zucchini!

Eggplant Fans with Onion Marmalade

Mild and nutty eggplant is the perfect backdrop for sweet onion marmalade and cool, creamy goat cheese.

2 tablespoons olive oil
2 medium onions, thinly sliced
½ teaspoon salt
1 teaspoon sugar
½ cup balsamic vinegar
8 sun-dried tomatoes, julienned
4 Japanese eggplants, about 3 to 4 inches long*
4 teaspoons olive oil, *divided*
salt to taste
2 ounces goat cheese, in 4 slices
4 – 8 basil leaves, whole, for garnish
4 – 8 basil leaves, cut in chiffonade**

Heat 2 tablespoons olive oil in large heavy skillet over low heat. Add onions; sprinkle with salt and sugar. Caramelize onions over low heat, stirring frequently, about 30 minutes, until golden brown.

Pour vinegar over onions; increase the heat to high. Bring the mixture to a boil; remove from heat. Stir in sun-dried tomatoes. Cover and set aside to keep warm. *The recipe can be prepared up to 3 days in advance to this point, cover and refrigerate. Reheat to serve.*

Meanwhile, fan cut the eggplants as directed in the sidebar. Preheat grill or grill pan over high heat. Brush eggplants with remaining olive oil; sprinkle with salt. Grill them until tender. Center one eggplant on each of four warmed serving plates, mound with one quarter of the caramelized onions, then place a slice of goat cheese beside the eggplant on plates. Drizzle the warm vinegar drippings from the onion marmalade around the edges of each of the eggplants. Garnish with whole basil leaves and chiffonade. Serve warm.

Serves 4.

*Japanese eggplants are smaller and more elongated than our domestic varieties. They may be found in specialty markets or your local supermarket.

**For chiffonade technique, see sidebar on page 39.

Garlic Mashed Potatoes

Warm and creamy with the nutty bite of garlic, these potatoes present a twist to the ever-popular side dish.

2 pounds Russet or Yukon gold potatoes, peeled
2 teaspoons salt
2 tablespoons butter
3 cloves garlic, minced
1 cup milk, heated
1 teaspoon freshly minced parsley or chives
salt and white pepper to taste
hot pepper sauce to taste

Cut potatoes into equal size chunks, about ¾ inch to allow for even cooking. Place in large saucepan; cover with cold water. Cover pot; bring to boil over high heat. When water boils, add salt. Continue to boil, uncovered, until potatoes are fork tender, about 20 minutes.

While potatoes are cooking, in small pan or in microwave heat butter until it sizzles. Add garlic; cook just until fragrant. Stir in milk; heat through. Remove from heat; keep warm.

When potatoes are done, drain well. Immediately press hot potatoes through ricer into a large ovenproof mixing bowl or mash by hand. Continue mashing potatoes by hand, or whip with electric mixer, adding hot milk mixture to thin and smooth to desired consistency. Stir in parsley or chives. Season well with salt, pepper and hot pepper sauce. Serve piping hot.

The recipe can be prepared entirely in advance: To hold potatoes for up to two hours, place in 160° F oven, LOOSELY covered. If covered tightly, condensation will drip back into the potatoes, causing them to turn into a brick. Whisk potatoes before serving.

Serves 4 to 6.

**VARIATION: For roasted garlic mashed potatoes, roast garlic according to recipe at sidebar. Substitute roasted garlic for fresh minced, proceed with recipe.

**VARIATION: For horseradish mashed potatoes, omit garlic; add 6 tablespoons prepared horseradish with the hot milk mixture.

**VARIATION: For wasabi mashed potatoes, omit garlic; mix 1 tablespoon wasabi powder with 1 tablespoon water, mix in with the hot milk mixture.

THE RIGHT TOOLS

RICERS

Potato ricers look like large garlic presses. The bowl of the ricer holds from 1 to 2 cups of potato chunks, which are then pressed through the small holes making the potatoes resemble rice. The potatoes will be perfectly smooth with very little effort.

Better quality ricers come with interchangeable discs. Use the smaller holes for smooth potatoes, and the larger holes for potatoes with more texture.

A ricer can be used to press spaetzle, sweet potatoes, eggplant, or other soft foods. Ricers are sold in quality kitchenware shops.

EXTRA TOUCHES

ROASTED GARLIC

To roast garlic, first remove the papery outer skin from the garlic heads, leaving the clusters of cloves intact. Cut a large slice off tip end of garlic, exposing some of the garlic in each clove. Place the garlic in the center of a sheet of aluminum foil. Dot each head with 1/2 teaspoon butter; sprinkle with salt and pepper. Wrap foil around garlic and seal. Roast at 350°F. for 1 hour, until garlic heads are golden brown and tender. To use, simply squeeze the garlic out of the browned husk. Store refrigerated.

KNOW YOUR INGREDIENTS

WASABI

Wasabi is pale green Japanese horseradish. The powder can be found in the spice section of your supermarket.

Apple Cider Glazed
Pork Chops

The glaze is a mouth-watering combination of apple and vinegar, both sweet and tart; topping pork chops so tender, moist and succulent you'll want them again tomorrow! The thick cut chops are essential for this recipe, as the thin ones cook too quickly.

For brine:
1 (one gallon size) resealable plastic bag
½ cup lightly packed brown sugar
⅓ cup kosher salt
1 or 2 medium garlic cloves, minced
1 tablespoon freshly ground black pepper

4 thick cut pork chops, trimmed (*about 5 ounces each*)
1 – 2 tablespoons vegetable oil for frying

For glaze:
4 shallots, thinly sliced
1 tablespoon olive oil
½ teaspoon salt
1 cup apple cider or juice
1 cup white wine
1 teaspoon fresh rosemary, chopped
¼ teaspoon dried thyme
½ teaspoon dried oregano
½ teaspoon hot pepper sauce
1 tablespoon apple cider vinegar
½ teaspoon arrowroot
    or 1 teaspoon cornstarch
1 tablespoon white wine or water
salt to taste
2 tablespoons Calvados

thin slices of apple

2 tablespoons maple syrup, optional

KNOW YOUR INGREDIENTS

Kosher salt *is a coarse-grained salt that is usually additive-free, so there is no chemical after taste. Because of its crystal structure, it tends to be less salty than table salt. If you must substitute, use half the volume of table salt in place of the kosher salt.*

Arrowroot *is a fine powdered starch used for thickening, producing a clear, filmy sauce. It is best added as a slurry to the liquid for the sauce. Arrowroot sauces must be brought to a boil to thicken properly. Small jars of arrowroot can be found in the spice section of your supermarket.*

Calvados *is apple brandy, and can be found in most shops where brandy is sold.*

Dissolve sugar and salt in 1 cup hot water. Pour into a large resealable plastic bag with the garlic and pepper, adding an additional 3 cups cold water. Place resealable bag into shallow pan. Add pork chops to the brine. Seal the bag, pressing out as much air as possible. Brine chops in solution for one hour. Remove pork chops from brine, pat dry. *If you choose not to cook the chops immediately after brining, remove them from the brine; pat them dry with paper towels. Refrigerate them on a wire rack, uncovered to allow to dry for up to four hours.*

Meanwhile, begin preparing glaze: Caramelize shallots VERY SLOWLY in olive oil with a pinch of salt, about 15 minutes. Add apple juice, 1 cup wine, half of the rosemary, thyme, oregano, hot pepper sauce, and vinegar. Over high heat, reduce to ½ cup. Make slurry by mixing arrowroot or cornstarch and the tablespoon of wine or water *(see the sidebar at the right)*. Add to reduced sauce mixture, bring to boil, to thicken slightly, then remove from heat. Correct seasonings. Set aside.

Preheat oven to 450°F. Place in the oven to preheat, a shallow pan large enough to hold the chops in a single layer. In a large skillet, heat oil over medium high heat. Sauté chops in skillet about two minutes per side, until crust forms. Brush presentation or top side with maple syrup if desired. Transfer chops to heated pan in preheated oven, roast to internal temperature of 125-127°F.

While chops are roasting, deglaze pork chop pan by adding the glaze mixture to the drippings in the pan; heat to boil. Stir in Calvados if desired, place apple slices and remaining rosemary in glaze to just heat through. Remove chops from oven, cover with foil. Let rest until internal temperature reaches 145°F, about 5 minutes. Serve on heated plates, topped with glaze. Garnish with apple slices and fresh rosemary, if desired. Serve with garlic mashed potatoes.

Serves 4.

COOKING CLASS

SLURRIES

A **slurry** is simply a mixture of some sort of starch, i.e. flour, cornstarch or arrowroot, which is mixed with a bit of **cold** liquid before being added to a hot sauce. The starch is for thickening the sauce, but if added directly to the hot sauce, it will form lumps. By making a slurry and adding it to the hot sauce, you will have a beautiful lump-free result.

COOKING CLASS

BRINING

Why do we **brine** *these chops? To make them moist and tender! The salt in the brine solution causes the proteins in the meat to unwind a bit, or denature, trapping extra water and flavors from the brine. The result — a juicy, succulent, flavorful chop!*

But a good thing can be overdone, so brine these chops for no more than an hour.

Fresh herbs are almost always preferable to dry, because of their fresher flavor. When fresh herbs are not available, you can use dried, but remember that the water content has been greatly reduced, concentrating the herb. A good rule of thumb is that one part dried herb is equal to three parts fresh.

When herbs are dried, the essential oils are locked inside. After measuring, if you place them in the palm of your hand, and rub the herbs between your hands while adding to your dish, you will release more of these essential oils, adding more flavor to your food.

These oils give the herbs their characteristic scents and flavors.

As dried herbs age, the essential oils eventually dry up. If the herbs in your pantry have very little aroma, it's time to replace them. They rarely last longer than a year.

Roasted Tomatoes Provençal

The meatiness of Roma or plum tomatoes is preferred for this dish, the juices won't dilute the flavors of the filling.

2 firm, ripe tomatoes, 3 – 4" in diameter (½ *pound*)
1 teaspoon salt
1 clove garlic, minced
1 tablespoon minced shallot
8 – 10 basil leaves, cut in chiffonade *(see sidebar on p. 39)*
    or 2 teaspoons dried basil
¼ teaspoon thyme or ¾ teaspoon fresh thyme
⅛ teaspoon salt
½ cup dry white bread crumbs *(see sidebar on p. 67)*
2 tablespoons olive oil
½ teaspoon pepper

Preheat oven to 400°F. Core tomatoes, then cut in half crosswise. Cut a very thin slice off the bottom of each tomato to allow it to stand upright. With your finger, press the seeds out of the cavities. Sprinkle the halves lightly with the 1 teaspoon salt and turn upside-down to drain on paper towels for 20 minutes or more.

Meanwhile, in a medium bowl, blend the garlic, shallots, basil, thyme, salt, breadcrumbs and 1 tablespoon of the olive oil. Taste and correct the seasonings. Sprinkle the inside of each tomato half with black pepper, then fill with a spoonful or two of the bread mixture. Drizzle the remaining olive oil over the filled tomatoes. Arrange the tomatoes in an oiled baking dish just large enough to hold them. *They can be prepared up to this point several hours ahead. Cover and refrigerate until ready to continue. Bring to room temperature before proceeding.*

Place the uncovered baking dish in the upper third of the preheated oven and roast the tomatoes for 10 to 15 minutes or until tender but still holding their shape. The breadcrumb filling should be slightly browned. *The tomatoes may be prepared ahead, then held in a 160°F oven for 30 minutes after cooking.* Serve hot or warm.

Serves 4.

*For a different flavor and aroma, replace the basil with 2 teaspoons sage.

Molten Chocolate Cakes

Just about everyone I know loves chocolate, warm and gooey, rich chocolate. Accented with fresh fruit these cakes are simple, elegant, satiating. Mmmm, you can cut this recipe in half to make a sensual dessert for two!

2 teaspoons butter, melted
4 ounces semi-sweet chocolate, chopped
4 ounces unsalted butter
2 whole eggs, at room temperature
2 yolks, at room temperature
¼ cup sugar
3 tablespoons flour
1 tablespoon cocoa powder

For garnish and presentation:
½ cup fruit coulis *(see recipe on p. 152)*
    or 4 – 6 tablespoons confectioner's sugar or cocoa powder
whipped cream
fresh berries and mint leaves

Preheat oven to 450°F. Using the 2 teaspoons melted butter, generously grease four 6-ounce ramekins or custard cups; place on baking sheet or shallow pan, set aside.

In saucepan over low heat or in microwave, melt chocolate and butter, set aside until just warm to the touch. Whip eggs, yolks and sugar until a ribbon trail forms *(see sidebar)*. Combine flour and cocoa powder. Sift half of the flour mixture over egg mixture; fold in using a whisk. Repeat with the remaining flour mixture. Fold in melted chocolate and butter. Spoon chocolate mixture into prepared ramekins or custard cups. *You can prepare this recipe up to 8 hours ahead to this point. Cover and chill ramekins until ready to bake. Allow the ramekins to stand at room temperature 20 to 30 minutes before baking.*

Bake in preheated oven 6 to 8 minutes. The cakes will still be very soft on top, and should be soft and gooey in the middle. Remove from oven; let cool 3 to 5 minutes. Meanwhile, prepare the plates: make a puddle of fruit coulis slightly off-center in each of 4 serving plates or dust the plates lightly with confectioner's sugar or cocoa in a fine sieve. Unmold cakes from ramekins by tipping out into an inverted plate, shaking the ramekin gently if necessary to loosen the cake. Dust the top of each cake with confectioner's sugar or cocoa. Place each cake to the side of the puddle of coulis, or slightly off center on the prepared plates. Garnish each with a whipped cream rosette, fresh berries and a sprig of mint. Serve warm.

Serves 4.

COOKING CLASS

WHAT IS A RIBBON TRAIL?

*This procedure can be accomplished by hand, but I recommend an electric mixer for the best result. Whisk the eggs and sugar at medium-low speed for the first minute, then increase the speed to high for about 4 to 6 minutes more. The mixture will become lighter in color and texture, and increase in volume dramatically. A **ribbon trail** is formed when you lift the beater from the mixture, and a smooth, thick stream drops from the beater into the bowl. The stream drops into the bowl leaving a trail that looks like a ribbon.*

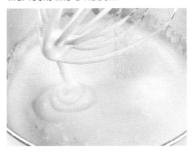

The eggs will beat faster and acquire more volume if they are at room temperature, rather than cold from the refrigerator.

***Folding** in the flour is best accomplished in this recipe using a whisk, to separate the flour and not break the air bubbles you have created in the egg mixture. Drag the whisk down through the center of mixture to the bottom of the bowl, then using a rotating wrist motion bring it back up the side of the bowl, "folding" the mixture over on itself.*

Rotate the bowl a quarter turn; repeat until the mixture is well combined.

Winter

Play in the bright, cold winter sun,
enjoy the snow. Brighten up the long
nights of winter — light a fire, light some
candles, invite some friends in to share
a hearty meal. Time to turn to the
comfort foods, warm and soothing.

Coriander and Pepper Crusted Salmon
with Mango Salsa
Sunomono Cucumbers

Ginger Cake

Lemon Filled Cakes

Goat Cheese & Sun-Dried Tomato Tart
Pear & Gorgonzola Salad

Panna Cotta with Truly Decadent Chocolate Sauce

Baked Brie with Toasts

Sautéed Prawns and Pineapple with Chili Oil Sauce

Banana Bread Pudding

Winter Menus

SIMPLE MELLOW FARE

Onion & Sage Spread with Crackers

Coriander and Pepper Crusted Salmon with Mango Salsa

Sunomono Cucumbers

Ginger Cake

REPAST FOR A FROSTY EVENING

Basil & Ricotta Tart

Cream of Tomato Bisque with Horseradish Cream

Tarragon Mushroom Salad

Lemon Filled Cakes

FIRESIDE LATE NIGHT SUPPER

Goat Cheese and Sun-Dried Tomato Tart

Pear & Gorgonzola Salad with Walnut Vinaigrette

Panna Cotta with Strawberries in Balsamic Vinegar

or Truly Decadent Chocolate Sauce

CELEBRATE THE SILVERY SOLSTICE

Baked Brie with Toasts

Sautéed Prawns and Pineapple with Chili Oil Sauce

Thai Jasmine Rice

Matchstick Carrot Bundles

Banana Bread Pudding

Simple Mellow Fare

Onion & Sage Spread with Crackers

◆

Coriander and Pepper Crusted Salmon
with
Mango Salsa

Sunomono Cucumbers

Breads
(purchased)

Chardonnay

◆

Gingercake

◆

Coffee and Tea

Simple Mellow Fare

Three days ahead:
Bake **Ginger Cake**. Cool, wrap tightly and freeze.
Fold the napkins if desired.

Two days ahead:
Prepare **Onion & Sage Spread**. Cover and chill.

The day before:
Put butter on its serving plate or bowl, cover and refrigerate.
Chill the wine and other cold beverages.
Set up coffee or tea tray, after dinner drinks, glasses, etc.
Make ice.
Set the table. Put out any non-food items (salt and pepper, wine coaster, etc.)
Arrange the flowers.

The morning before:
Prepare **Mango Salsa**, cover and refrigerate.
Peel and slice cucumbers for **Sunomono Cucumbers**. Salt and refrigerate.
Prepare spice mixture for **Coriander and Pepper Crusted Salmon**. Set aside.
Remove **Ginger Cake** from freezer to thaw.
Set up coffee maker.

6 hours before guests arrive:
Drain and squeeze water from **Sunomono Cucumbers**, add vinegar; refrigerate. Prepare dressing, set aside.
Trim, dry and crust the fish with the spice mixture for **Coriander and Pepper Crusted Salmon**. Cover and chill.
Spoon **Onion & Sage Spread** into small serving bowl; Cover and chill.

1 – 2 hours before guests arrive:
Drain cucumbers for **Sunomono Cucumbers**. Toss with dressing, chill.
Slice **Ginger Cake** into wedges for serving. Whip cream for garnish; refrigerate.
Remove butter from refrigerator to soften.
Slice purchased bread, if serving.

Before your guests arrive:
Preheat the oven and the baking sheet for **Coriander and Pepper Crusted Salmon**.
Arrange crackers and **Onion & Sage Spread** on serving tray.
Preheat the plates and platters as needed.

After the guests arrive:
Sauté and roast the **Coriander and Pepper Crusted Salmon**, serve on warmed plates.
Plate the entree and accompaniments.
Plate the **Ginger Cake**, garnish.

KNOW YOUR INGREDIENTS

ONIONS

There are hundreds of varieties of onions which are classified in two categories: fresh or sweet vs. storage or dry.

Fresh or sweet onions are those which mature in summer, including Walla Walla, Maui, Vidalia and scallions. Due to their high water and sugar content they should be used quickly, as they do not keep well.

Storage or dry onions are available during fall and winter. They have a higher sulfur content making them taste and smell stronger, with the traditional onion heat. They keep well in a cool dry place for up to three months.

Once revered for their medicinal properties, onions are once again being studied for their health benefits. Onions are quite nutritious, providing fiber and anti-oxidants, as well as good sources of vitamin C, potassium and calcium.

Onion & Sage Spread

1 slice bacon, finely diced
1 pound yellow onions (2 medium), sliced thinly
½ teaspoon sugar
¼ teaspoon salt
1 teaspoon balsamic vinegar
1 tablespoon finely chopped fresh sage
freshly ground black pepper

Over medium heat sauté bacon until almost crisp. Add onions, salt and sugar. Cook until onions are caramelized, about 15 to 20 minutes, stirring frequently. Stir in sage, vinegar and pepper; set aside. *May be prepared two days in advance and refrigerated. Bring to room temperature before serving*

Serve on wheat crackers.

Makes about ¾ cup spread.

Coriander and Pepper Crusted Salmon

Fresh salmon is becoming more readily available across the country. In the Pacific Northwest, salmon is a staple. It is most likely the easiest of seafood to prepare because of the high fat content, making it less likely to dry out in the cooking process. The spice of the coriander and pepper combined with the richness of the salmon juxtapose the cool, refreshing mango salsa, each demanding attention.

4 teaspoons whole coriander seeds
1 teaspoon coarsely ground black pepper
1 teaspoon salt
1 tablespoon freshly minced coriander or cilantro leaves

4 salmon fillets (*about 4 ounces each*)
2 tablespoons olive oil
salt

With a mortar and pestle, or the back of a large spoon in a small bowl, crush the coriander seeds. Combine with the pepper, salt and coriander leaves. *This may be done 6 hours in advance. Cover and set aside.*

Preheat oven and baking sheet to 425°F. Spread coriander and pepper mixture on shallow plate. Lightly brush each salmon fillet with ½ teaspoon olive oil; press into spice mixture to coat only the topside. *The salmon can be prepared to this point in advance, covered and refrigerated for up to 6 hours. Let salmon rest for 15 minutes to come to room temperature before cooking.*

Heat remaining oil in sauté pan over high heat. Place fillets in heated pan, cook 2 minutes on each side. Remove to heated baking sheet. Place in preheated oven; cook 5 to 10 minutes, until internal temperature reaches 135°F.

Remove from oven, tent with foil. Let stand 2 to 4 minutes, until internal temperature reaches 145° F. Serve immediately, with mango salsa.

Serves 4.

Variation:

Delete coating salmon with coriander and pepper mixture. Brush with oil; sear salmon as directed above. Before roasting, brush top of each fillet with 1 teaspoon maple syrup, sprinkle lightly with black pepper. Continue as above.

EXTRA TOUCHES

MANGO SALSA

1 ripe mango
½ small red onion, finely diced
2 tablespoons cilantro, minced
2 tablespoons red bell pepper, finely diced
½ teaspoon ground cumin
red pepper flakes (optional)
salt and pepper to taste

Puree half of mango in food processor or blender. Dice remaining half. Gently stir all ingredients together to combine, season to taste. Store refrigerated.

KNOW YOUR INGREDIENTS

CORIANDER

Coriander is commonly found in a variety of cuisines, from Mexican to Indian, from Scandinavian to Chinese. But it can be bewildering, first because fresh coriander is also known as cilantro, Mexican or Chinese parsley. Second because we use the fresh leaves as an herb, but the dried seeds as a spice. And third, the flavor of the leaves bears no resemblance to the spice!

Fresh coriander is found in the produce section of your market. To store, make a fresh cut at the bottom of the stem, stand the herbs in a small glass of water. Store refrigerated for up to a week.

Coriander seeds are most often found ground, in the spice section. Larger gourmet stores, those with bulk food departments or specialty spice shops carry whole seeds.

Pale yellow Japanese rice vinegar is made from fermented rice. Also known as rice wine vinegar, it is considerably milder than American or European vinegars, with a slight sweetness.

Seasoned rice vinegar has been flavored with salt, and possible other seasonings. Either type will work well in this recipe, but I prefer to add my own seasoning, so I use the unseasoned variety.

You can find Japanese rice vinegar either in the Asian section of your market, or with the vinegars.

Sunomono Cucumbers

In Japan salads prepared with vinegar are known as "Sunomono." Crisp and crunchy, these cucumbers are slightly sweet, and slightly tart. The cool pale green accents the salmon and mango salsa. Your dinner plate will be a work of art.

2 cucumbers, peeled and sliced very thin
1 teaspoon salt
¼ cup white or cider vinegar

For dressing:

4 tablespoons Japanese rice vinegar
3 tablespoons sugar (superfine sugar will dissolve more easily)
½ teaspoon salt
½ teaspoon freshly grated ginger

Place cucumbers in a sieve or colander over a bowl. Toss with the 1 teaspoon salt. Let stand 30 minutes to an hour. Squeeze as much liquid from the cucumbers as you can, then wrap in a double layer of paper towels and squeeze again.

Pour white or cider vinegar over cucumbers and let stand 30 minutes to an hour more in refrigerator. Drain well. Meanwhile, mix all ingredients for dressing together. When cucumbers are drained, pour dressing over. Toss well. Chill until serving time.

This recipe may be made six hours ahead, and stored in refrigerator until serving time.

Serves 4.

Variation: Up to one hour before serving time, toss the cucumbers with one 7-ounce can crab or shrimp, drained and rinsed.

Ginger Cake

While studying at Le Cordon Bleu in London, I had the good fortune to work with Chef John Power. His skill as a pastry chef is unmatched. His gingerbread has inspired this recipe.

2½ cups self-rising flour
2 teaspoons baking soda
1½ tablespoons ground ginger
1½ teaspoons ground cinnamon
1½ teaspoons ground allspice
¾ cup unsalted butter, at room temperature
1½ cups milk
¾ cup brown sugar
½ cup molasses
½ cup dark corn syrup
4 tablespoons vegetable oil
1 egg
⅓ cup coarsely chopped pecans
⅓ cup coconut

whipped cream, for garnish

Preheat oven to 350°F. You may bake this recipe in an 8-inch round pan with 2-inch sides, or a standard 9-inch round pan. Line your choice of pan as directed in the sidebar. Set aside.

In large mixing bowl, sift together flour, baking soda, ginger, cinnamon and allspice. Cut in butter until it resembles the size of peas. Set aside.

In small saucepan over low heat, cook milk and brown sugar until sugar is completely dissolved. Add molasses and corn syrup, heat and stir until smooth. Cool until just warm to the touch. Stir in the oil and egg.

Whisk milk mixture into the sifted dry ingredients. Mix well. Pour into prepared pan. Combine pecans and coconut. Gently sprinkle the nut mixture over the top of the batter. Place in preheated oven. If during baking the nuts and coconut begin to darken too much, lay a sheet of aluminum foil across the top of the cake. Bake 30 to 45 minutes, until top springs back when pressed lightly. When the cake is done, remove from oven, cool on rack.

Cover the top of cake with a sheet of waxed paper and a plate. Gently invert cake, remove the pan and the bottom paper. Invert onto serving plate. Cut into wedges. Garnish with whipped cream rosettes.

Serves 8.

COOKING CLASS

Lining a baking pan with parchment paper *takes a little more time in the preparation, but assures success in removing the cake from the pan easily.*

First, place the pan on the parchment, trace the bottom. Cut out the desired shape and trim slightly smaller.

Grease the bottom of the pan; this will hold the parchment in place as you finish.

Place the parchment in the bottom of the pan; press firmly to affix the paper.

Then grease the paper and the sides of the pan.

To remove the cake from the pan after it has cooled, run a small knife around the edge to loosen the cake from sides of the pan. Invert the pan onto a plate or wire rack. Gently lift the pan away from the cake, and peel away the paper.

Repast for a Frosty Evening

Basil and Ricotta Tart

◆

Cream of Tomato Bisque
with
Horseradish Cream

Tarragon Mushroom Salad

French Bread
(purchased)

*Pinot Noir or
Sauvignon Blanc*

◆

Lemon Filled
Cakes

◆

Coffee and Tea

Repast for a Frosty Evening

Three days ahead:
Prepare pastry, roll and place in tart pan for **Basil and Ricotta Tart**. Freeze pastry.
Prepare **Lemon Curd**; refrigerate.
Fold the napkins if desired.

Two days ahead:
Prepare **Cream of Tomato Bisque**. Cover and refrigerate.

The day before:
Shop for fruit garnish for **Lemon Filled Cakes**.
Blind bake pastry shell for **Basil and Ricotta Tart**. Cool, cover and set aside. Prepare filling, cover and refrigerate.
Prepare cake for **Lemon Filled Cakes**. Cover and set aside.
Prepare mushrooms for **Tarragon Mushroom Salad**. Wash and dry greens. Chill.
Put butter on its serving plate or bowl, cover and refrigerate.
Chill the wine and other cold beverages.
Set up coffee or tea tray, after dinner drinks, glasses, etc.
Make ice.
Set the table. Put out any non-food items (salt and pepper, wine coaster, etc.)
Arrange the flowers.

The morning before:
Cut strawberries for garnish of **Lemon Filled Cakes**. Cover and refrigerate.
Cut and fill cakes for **Lemon Filled Cakes**. Cover and refrigerate. Dust plates with confectioner's sugar, set aside.
Wash and dry greens for **Tarragon Mushroom Salad**.
Set up coffee maker.

1 – 2 hours before guests arrive:
Whip cream for both **Horseradish Cream** and for dessert garnish. Into one-half cup, stir in horseradish. Reserve
   remaining whipped cream for dessert. Cover and refrigerate both creams.
One hour before, spread filling into prebaked shell for **Basil and Ricotta Tart**. Bake as directed.
Remove butter from refrigerator to soften.
Slice purchased bread, if serving.

Before your guests arrive:
Slice **Basil and Ricotta Tart** into wedges for serving.
Rewarm the **Cream of Tomato Bisque**.
Plate the **Tarragon Mushroom Salad**.
Preheat the plates and platters as needed.

After the guests arrive:
Stir the Madeira into **Cream of Tomato Bisque**; serve.
At serving time, plate **Lemon Filled Cakes**. Complete garnish and serve.

ROLLING PASTRY

If you struggle to roll pastry because it sticks to the rolling surface or rolling pin, or if you just can't get it into the pan here are a few tips from the pros:

Although the recipe on the right does not require chilling most others recommend it. So, if you are using another recipe, make sure the dough has been well chilled before attempting to roll it. The hardened butter will be much less sticky, and the dough will hold together more easily.

After kneading the dough to even out the temperature, roll it into a ball and then flatten into a disk. Smooth the edges, then begin rolling with the pin.

Your rolling surface should be DRY and lightly dusted with flour. Rub a bit of flour on the rolling pin as well.

Place the flattened pastry disk in the center of your surface. Begin to roll from the center out. Roll toward you, then away. Lift the dough, slide and rotate it 90°. Then roll toward yourself, and away. Continue rolling, sliding and turning. You may need to occasionally add a bit of flour to the rolling surface.

When dough is desired size and thickness hold the rolling pin near one edge. Fold the edge of the pastry over the rolling pin. Hold the pin above the pastry and carefully roll the pastry onto the rolling pin. Transfer to the pan unrolling the pastry sheet from one side to the other. Shape and chill in the freezer at least 15 minutes.

Basil and Ricotta Tart

A very flavorful and unique addition to your appetizer repartee. This is a great recipe to double, freezing the extra tart for another use. The pastry recipe is by far the easiest to work that I have ever found because it does not require chilling before it is rolled. And the result is flaky and tasty as ever.

pastry for TWO 8" tarts:
1⅓ cup flour
½ teaspoon salt
10 tablespoons butter, CHILLED, cut in small cubes
4 to 5 tablespoons ice water

Sift flour and salt. Add butter cubes to flour, cut in until pieces are about half the size of a pea *(see sidebar on p. 20)*. By hand add 3 tablespoons ice water; bring mixture together with scraper. Add more water very slowly as necessary, taking care not to add too much. The dough should not be sticky or too soft to handle. Divide dough into two equal portions; shape into two balls, flatten into disks. If the dough is reasonably cool, you may work it immediately, or wrap and chill at 15 minutes. *If you are preparing only one tart, freeze remaining pastry up to 2 months for another use.*

On a lightly floured surface flatten and roll pastry, each time ROLL, SLIDE and TURN. Add flour as necessary. Check thickness; roll to ⅛ inch. Roll pastry around rolling pin; transfer to lightly greased tart pan. Cut off bit of excess, roll in flour, and use as a "pusher" to press edges to side of pan. Trim top with rolling pin. Go around top edge of pastry with thumb pushing up "thumbing up." Chill on tray in the freezer 30 minutes. Prick bottom and sides of pastry shell with fork.

**To blind bake: Preheat oven to 375°F. Line pastry shell with baking cartouche *(see sidebar on p. 69)*. Fill with pie weights, pressing out to edge of pastry. Bake until edges are golden brown, about 10 minutes. Remove pie weights and cartouche. Return to oven; continue baking 3 to 4 minutes longer. Pastry is done when bottom is dry. Cool on rack.

Filling for one 8" pastry shell:
⅔ cup fresh basil, or combination of basil and fresh spinach
2 teaspoons fresh parsley
1 teaspoon olive oil
1 cup ricotta cheese
2 tablespoons freshly grated Parmesan
1 egg
salt and pepper

Process basil and parsley in food processor until coarsely chopped. Add oil, ricotta, Parmesan, process just until mixed. Add egg, salt and pepper to taste. Pour mixture into cooled pastry shell, distributing evenly. Bake at 375°F for 25 to 30 minutes, or until knife inserted in center comes out clean. Cut into wedges, serve at room temperature. *May be prepared one day in advance and refrigerated or frozen for 2 months.*

Serves 4 to 6.

Cream of Tomato Bisque

And what is bisque? Simply put, it is thick, rich soup made with pureed vegetables or seafood, and cream. This one is silky smooth, rich and elegant, and can be presented as a first course, or as the basis for a hearty meal. A word of caution: I have had hot food burst out of the blender, so be sure to follow the blending directions carefully.

¼ cup butter
½ cup chopped celery
½ cup chopped onion
¼ cup chopped carrots
3 tablespoons flour
1 (28-ounce) can whole or chopped tomatoes
2 cups chicken stock or
    1 (15-ounce) can low-sodium broth
1 teaspoon sugar
½ teaspoon dried basil
½ teaspoon marjoram
1 bay leaf
½ cup heavy cream
¼ teaspoon paprika
¼ teaspoon curry powder
⅛ – ¼ teaspoon salt
⅛ teaspoon white pepper
1 tablespoon Madeira
horseradish cream *(see sidebar for recipe)*
freshly chopped chives

Over medium heat, melt butter in a large, heavy covered saucepan; sauté celery, onions and carrots until tender but not browned. Add flour; cook 2 to 3 minutes, stirring constantly. Add tomatoes, stock, sugar, basil, marjoram, and bay leaf. Bring mixture to a boil, then lower heat, cover and simmer 30 minutes uncovered, stirring occasionally. Remove and discard bay leaf.

Taking care to fill blender jar no more than half-full, ladle hot soup mixture into blender jar. Hold the lid on the jar tightly with a pot holder or kitchen towel. THEN turn on the blender at low speed. Increase the speed to puree the soup to desired consistency. For velvety smooth soup, strain through a sieve. Continue processing the soup in batches until all has been pureed.

Return the soup to the pan, over low heat. Add cream, paprika, curry powder, salt and pepper; stir to blend. Correct the seasonings. *The soup can be made 2 days in advance and refrigerated or frozen for up to six months. Reheat to serve.*

Just before serving, stir in the Madeira, if desired. Serve hot, topped with a dollop of horseradish cream and sprinkled with chopped chives.

Makes about 6 cups soup, four main course portions or eight first course servings.

EXTRA TOUCHES

HORSERADISH CREAM

¹/₂ cup whipped cream
2 teaspoons fresh horseradish
pinch of salt

Fold horseradish into whipped cream, season with salt.

KNOW YOUR INGREDIENTS

STOCK OR BROTH

So, what's the difference between **stock and broth**? *Simply put, a stock is made with the meat, fish or poultry of choice, with vegetables added for flavor. A broth is made from the meat, fish or poultry only, no vegetables. The classic vegetables of choice are carrots, celery and onions, which add a tremendous amount of flavor to stock. I prefer stock.* **Bouillon** *is the same as stock.*

If you prefer to make your own stock see recipes on p. 171-173.

Most herbs don't retain their bright, fresh flavor after drying, but tarragon is an exception to the rule. To rehydrate the herb, simply place the dried leaves in a bowl, and cover with tepid water. Let stand 5 minutes, then drain. The fresh, distinctive anise-like flavor is reborn.

Tarragon Mushroom Salad

2 tablespoons butter
1 – 2 cloves garlic, minced
1 pound sliced fresh mushrooms
1 tablespoon fresh tarragon, snipped,
    or 1 teaspoon dried, rehydrated *(see sidebar at left)*
juice of one fresh lemon
salt and pepper to taste
one head butter lettuce, washed and dried

In skillet, heat butter over medium heat, add garlic, sauté until fragrant. Add mushrooms and tarragon, sauté just until mushrooms are tender. Sprinkle liberally with lemon juice, salt and pepper to taste; cool. *The mushrooms may be prepared one day in advance.*

Meanwhile, tear lettuce and divide among 4 salad plates. Top each with mushroom mixture, serve.

Serves 4.

Lemon Filled Cakes

Garnish as desired, and wow everyone with your presentation! These are easily prepared with items normally found in your pantry.

1 pkg. yellow or white cake mix (*18-¼ ounces*),
    mixed according to directions,
      OR one full recipe of your favorite cake** see below
¾ cup lemon curd (*recipe follows*)
confectioner's sugar
fresh strawberries for garnish
strawberry puree for garnish (*see recipe on p. 152*)
whipping cream, for garnish

Mix cake mix according to package directions or prepare your favorite cake recipe batter. Line bottoms of **TWO 9 x 13 inch pans with parchment paper, butter and flour pan and paper (*see sidebar on p. 89*). Divide cake batter evenly between pans; spread to even out. Bake until done. (Baking time should be about one-half to two-thirds that listed for one 9 x 13 inch cake.) Cool on rack about 10 minutes, remove from pans, cool completely. Carefully peel away parchment paper. *The cake can be prepared one day ahead, covered and set aside. Do not refrigerate, as it will dry out. Or, place in an airtight container and freeze for up to two months.*

With circular, heart or other shaped cutter, cut cake into desired shapes. Spread half of the cutouts with very thin coat of curd; stack a second cutout on top. Dust with confectioner's sugar.

For presentation, dust plate with confectioner's sugar. If you choose rounds, cut cake round in half, place half on garnished plate, lean other half at an angle. Garnish with whipped cream rosette and fruit. Serve immediately.

Or, puddle fruit puree or sauce on plate, make design with second sauce or puree. Place cake heart off center; garnish with fruit and whipped cream if desired. Serve immediately.

Try this recipe with other combinations of cake and jams or jellies, for example: chocolate or Devil's food cake with raspberry jam dusted with cocoa powder instead of confectioner's sugar, white cake with strawberry preserves, or gingerbread with apple jelly. Your imagination is the only limit!

TIMESAVER!

Or, you can make this dessert even more simply by using a purchased poundcake, slicing it ½ to ¾ inch thick. Proceed with your cutters and jam.

Lemon Curd

I learned to make this wonderfully easy lemon curd while living in London. It is an essential part of the menu for High Tea, with scones. It's so quick you can make it anytime with ingredients you normally have on hand.

Finely grated zest and juice of 1 lemon
½ cup sugar
1 egg, beaten then strained
2 tablespoons butter, cut into small cubes

Place all the ingredients in a large heatproof bowl and mix well. Cook in the microwave on high power for 1 minute. Stir well and cook for a further minute. Repeat until the mixture just begins to thicken, then cook at 30-second intervals until it coats the back of a wooden spoon. This takes 1 to 3 minutes, depending on the temperature of your ingredients and the wattage of your microwave. Take care the mixture doesn't boil or it will curdle.

Remove from heat. Pour into a jar and seal tightly. Allow to cool, then refrigerate. *The curd will store about 3 weeks.*

Makes about 2 cups.

Lime curd:

Replace lemon juice with juice of one half lemon, and juice of one half lime. Replace lemon zest with zest of one lime.

Orange curd:

Replace lemon juice with juice of one half lemon, and juice of one half orange. Replace lemon zest with zest of one orange.

Raspberry curd:

Replace lemon juice with juice of one half lemon, and 1½ tablespoons raspberry puree. *(see recipe on p. 152)*

This recipe makes more than needed to fill the cakes. Just seal the remaining curd, and refrigerate. Use for spreading on toasted English muffins, biscuits or scones at breakfast. It is also a terrific filling for tartlets.

Fireside Late Night Supper

Goat Cheese and
Sun-Dried Tomato Tart

Pear and Gorgonzola Salad
with
Walnut Vinaigrette

Breads
(purchased)

*Pinot Gris or
Sauvignon Blanc*

◆

Panna Cotta
with
Strawberries in Balsamic Vinegar
or
Truly Decadent Chocolate Sauce

◆

Coffee and Tea

Fireside Late Night Supper

Three days ahead:
Fold the napkins if desired.
Prepare pastry, roll and place in tart pan for **Goat Cheese and Sun-Dried Tomato Tart**. Freeze pastry.
Prepare **Truly Decadent Chocolate Sauce** for **Panna Cotta** if desired.

Two days ahead:
Prepare **Panna Cotta** (use ½ package gelatin). Cover and chill.

The day before:
Shop for strawberries for **Panna Cotta** if using.
Blind bake pastry shell for **Goat Cheese and Sun-Dried Tomato Tart**, cool. Arrange cheese and tomatoes in shell, cover and chill. Prepare egg filling, cover and refrigerate separately.
Prepare dressing for **Pear and Gorgonzola Salad.** Crumble Gorgonzola cheese; cover and refrigerate separately.
Put butter on its serving plate or bowl, cover and refrigerate.
Chill the wine and other cold beverages.
Set up coffee or tea tray, after dinner drinks, glasses, etc.
Make ice.
Set the table. Put out any non-food items (salt and pepper, wine coaster, etc.)
Arrange the flowers.

The morning before:
Wash and dry greens for **Pear and Gorgonzola Salad**. Place in large bowl, cover and refrigerate.
Set up coffee maker.

6 hours before guests arrive:
Prepare **Strawberries in Balsamic Vinegar** if using, or prepare any fresh fruit garnish for **Panna Cotta** if desired.

1 – 2 hours before guests arrive:
Unmold **Panna Cotta** onto serving plates if desired. Keep chilled.
Remove butter from refrigerator to soften.
Slice purchased bread, if serving.

Before your guests arrive:
Preheat the plates and platters as needed.
One-half hour before, pour filling over cheese and tomatoes in prebaked shell, bake **Goat Cheese and Sun-Dried Tomato Tart** as directed. Slice into wedges.
For **Pear and Gorgonzola Salad** toss greens with dressing, divide onto serving plates. Slice pears, complete the salad. Place on serving table.

After the guests arrive:
At serving time, plate the **Panna Cotta**, serve with desired garnish.

BLIND BAKING
PASTRY SHELLS

Quite often I will choose to "blind bake" a pastry shell, meaning bake it without a filling. This is necessary if the filling is not to be cooked in the shell or not at all. It is also helpful for those tarts and pies whose crusts may become soggy during the cooking.

To blind bake a pastry shell, preheat oven to 375°F. Line pastry shell with baking cartouche (see sidebar on p. 62). Fill with pie weights, dried beans or rice, pressing out to edge of pastry. Bake until edges are golden brown, about 10 minutes. Remove pie weights and cartouche. Return pastry shell to oven; continue baking 3 to 4 minutes longer. Pastry is done when bottom is dry. Cool on rack

I like to blind bake the pastry for this tart before baking again with the filling because the crust then maintains its flaky crisp qualities. It makes a big difference in the finished product, and it can be completely finished the day before I want to fill and serve it!

Goat Cheese and Sun-Dried Tomato Tart

Pastry for 10" tart:
1⅓ cup flour
½ teaspoon salt
10 tablespoons butter, CHILLED, cut in small cubes
4 to 5 tablespoons ice water

Sift flour and salt. Add butter cubes to flour, cut in until pieces are about half the size of a pea *(see sidebar on p. 20)*. By hand add 3 tablespoons ice water; bring mixture together with scraper. Add more water very slowly as necessary, taking care not to add too much. The dough should not be sticky or too soft to handle. Shape the dough into a ball, flatten into a disk. If the dough is reasonably cool, you may work it immediately, or wrap and chill at 15 minutes.

On a lightly floured surface flatten and roll pastry, each time ROLL, SLIDE and TURN. Add flour as necessary. Check thickness, roll to ⅛ inch. Roll pastry around rolling pin; transfer to lightly greased tart pan. Cut off bit of excess, roll in flour, and use as a "pusher" to press edges to side of pan. Trim top with rolling pin. Go around top edge of pastry with thumb pushing up "thumbing up." Chill on tray in the freezer 30 minutes. Preheat oven to 375°F. Prick bottom and sides of pastry shell with fork. Blind bake the tart shell, remove from oven and let cool. Lower oven temperature to 300°F. Meanwhile, prepare filling:

For filling:
⅔ cup milk
⅔ cup creme fraiche or sour cream
3 eggs
½ teaspoon salt
¼ teaspoon hot pepper sauce, or ground pepper
¼ teaspoon freshly ground nutmeg
6 – 8 ounces goat cheese
¼ cup sun-dried tomatoes, drained and patted dry

Whisk together milk, cream, eggs and seasonings. Arrange slices of goat cheese in bottom of shell, sprinkle with tomatoes. *Tart may be assembled to this point one day ahead. Wrap and chill.* Pour egg mixture over cheese and tomatoes. Bake tart until set, about 30 to 45 minutes. Cut into wedges, serve hot.

Serves 6 to 8.

Pear and Gorgonzola Salad

For dressing:
2 tablespoons white wine vinegar or Champagne vinegar
¼ teaspoon salt
¼ teaspoon Dijon mustard
½ teaspoon fresh thyme, or ¼ teaspoon dried thyme
6 tablespoons walnut oil

4 cups mixed leafy salad greens, washed and dried
2 small very ripe pears
4 ounces Gorgonzola cheese, crumbled
¼ cup shelled walnuts
freshly ground black pepper

In small mixing bowl or blender container, combine vinegar, salt, mustard and thyme until salt has dissolved. Starting with a few drops at a time, slowly add the walnut oil, whisking or blending constantly. When one or two tablespoons of the oil have been incorporated into the mixture, you may add the oil slowly in a steady stream. Continue whisking or blending. The vinaigrette should thicken slightly as the last of the oil is added. *To prepare ahead, cover and store at room temperature up to 24 hours in advance. Whisk before using.*

Makes about ½ cup dressing.

Thinly slice pears *(see technique in sidebar on p. 120).*

Place salad greens in large bowl, toss with about 6 tablespoons of the dressing. Arrange greens on individual serving plates if desired. Top with pear slices; drizzle with remaining 2 tablespoons dressing. Sprinkle with Gorgonzola and walnuts, and freshly ground pepper if desired.

Thinly slice pears *(see technique in sidebar on p. 120).*

KNOW YOUR INGREDIENTS

GORGONZOLA CHEESE

Gorgonzola cheese, a northern Italian staple, is a rich blue cheese made of cow's milk. When young, it is mild and nutty, with a sweet, creamy texture. As the cheese ages, it becomes a bit more pungent with a slightly firmer texture. Use whichever type you prefer for this recipe.

Use a fork to crumble the cheese.

Look for creamy colored wedges with light blue or green veining.

Store the cheese in an airtight container in the refrigerator. It should keep for several weeks. You can find Gorgonzola in the deli section of your supermarket or at specialty cheese shops.

✓ Panna Cotta

EXTRA TOUCHES

STRAWBERRIES IN BALSAMIC VINEGAR

1 to 1 1/2 cups fresh strawberries
     quartered, sliced or very
     small sized berries
2 – 3 tablespoons sugar
1/4 teaspoon pure vanilla extract
2 tablespoons best quality
     balsamic vinegar

In medium bowl sprinkle berries with
sugar. Add vanilla and balsamic
vinegar. Set aside at room temperature to allow flavors to develop. Can
be prepared 6 to 8 hours in advance.

KNOW YOUR INGREDIENTS

GELATIN

As a gelatin mixture sets over time it
becomes firmer and can get
"rubbery," a quality you do not want
in your Panna Cotta. To balance this
effect, the amount of gelatin required
should be adjusted according to the
length of available setting time. A
short setting time of 24 hours or less
requires 1 package gelatin for this
recipe, a longer setting time requires
less gelatin, as little as 1/2 package.

Pronounced "pawn-a coat-a," the name means "Cooked Cream." I learned to make this dish from Judy Witts in Florence, Italy, where in spring this dish is prepared with tiny wild strawberries. You will be pleasantly surprised by the unique blend of strawberries and balsamic vinegar, highlighting the fresh qualities of the fruit. Plan to prepare the Panna Cotta in advance at least one day or as many as three.

2 cups whipping cream
     or for a lighter version, use 1 cup milk and 1 cup cream
1/4 cup sugar
seeds and pod from one vanilla bean *(see sidebar on p. 151)*
     or 1 teaspoon pure vanilla extract
1/2 to 1 package unflavored gelatin *(see sidebar for information)*

for garnish:
1 recipe Strawberries in Balsamic Vinegar and
fresh mint leaves
Or 1/4 cup Truly Decadent Chocolate Sauce *(see recipe on p. 150)* and
fresh strawberries or raspberries, or canned mandarin oranges

Pour about 1/4 cup cream into a small bowl, sprinkle the gelatin over. Allow the gelatin to soften as directed on package, about 5 minutes.

Meanwhile, heat remaining cream with vanilla seeds and pod over low heat. Add sugar, and stir until dissolved. Mixture should be warm, but not too hot to the touch. Remove the cream mixture from the heat. Stir in gelatin until melted. Do not let cream overheat with the gelatin, as heat will destroy the setting properties.

Strain mixture through a sieve to remove any gelatin lumps and the vanilla pod. Pour into 4 individual molds or goblets. Chill until set. Cover tightly with plastic wrap and store in refrigerator.

To serve molded Panna Cotta, dip molds in warm water for about 15 seconds. Run a small knife around the edge of the Panna Cotta to loosen. Invert onto serving plate, remove mold. Serve with Strawberries in Balsamic Vinegar *(see sidebar)* or surround with barely warmed Truly Decadent Chocolate Sauce and garnish with fresh fruit or mandarin orange segments.

To serve in goblets, top with small amount of strawberries in Balsamic Vinegar; garnish each with a mint leaf or two.

Serves 4.

Celebrate the Silvery Solstice

Baked Brie

Champagne,
Zinfandel or
Syrah

◆

Sautéed Tiger Prawns
and
Pineapple
with
Chili Oil Sauce

Thai Jasmine Rice
(See recipe in sidebar on p. 139)

Matchstick Carrot Bundles

Assorted Breads
(purchased)
Flavored Butter
(optional, see recipes in
"Show-Offs!!" section)

Gewertztraminer or
Riesling

◆

Banana Bread Pudding

◆

Coffee and Tea

Celebrate the Silvery Solstice

Four days ahead:
Prepare chili oil, if desired.
Prepare **Caramel Sauce** for **Banana Bread Pudding**.

Three days ahead:
Prepare **Flavored Butters**, if desired. Cover and refrigerate.
Fold the napkins if desired.

Two days ahead:
Wash and julienne cut carrots for **Matchstick Carrot Bundles**. Wrap with chives Steam the bundles and refresh. Wrap in
    plastic and refrigerate.
Prepare raspberry sauce for **Baked Brie**, cover and refrigerate.
Prepare **Creme Fraiche**, if desired. Set aside.

The day before:
Prepare the crème fraiche sauce for the **Sautéed Tiger Prawns**; cover and refrigerate.
Peel and slice the pineapple for the **Sautéed Tiger Prawns**. Cover and refrigerate.
Put the **Flavored Butter** on its serving plate or bowl, cover and refrigerate.
Chill the wine and other cold beverages.
Set up coffee or tea tray, after dinner drinks, glasses, etc.
Make ice.
Set the table. Put out any non-food items (salt and pepper, wine coaster, etc.)
Arrange the flowers.

The morning before:
Place cheese for **Baked Brie** in ovenproof serving dish; mound with sugar, dot with butter. Cover and refrigerate.
Prepare chili oil sauce for **Sautéed Tiger Prawns**; cover and set aside.
Clean and devein the prawns. Cover tightly and refrigerate.
Set up coffee maker.

5 hours ahead:
Prepare **Bread Pudding** mixture, spoon into ramekins, cover and refrigerate.

1 – 2 hours before guests arrive:
Slice and butter baguette for **Baked Brie**, place on baking sheet. Cover and set aside.
Prepare **Thai Jasmine Rice. Keep warm in 160°F oven.**
Remove flavored butter from refrigerator to soften.
Slice purchased bread, if serving.

Before your guests arrive:
Preheat the baking tray for the **Sautéed Tiger Prawns, as well as** the plates and platters as needed.
Simmer water to reheat carrot bundles.
Toast the baguette slices for **Baked Brie**; arrange on serving platter. Warm the raspberry sauce.
Bake the Brie, top with sauce and almonds. Surround with toasted baguette slices.
Remove caramel sauce from refrigerator to soften.
Preheat the oven for the **Bread Pudding**.

After the guests arrive:
Reheat the carrot bundles and the chili oil sauce.
Sauté the pineapple and prawns for **Sautéed Tiger Prawns. Keep warm in 160°F oven.**
Stir the rice and plate the entrée.
Bake **Banana Bread Pudding**.
Warm **Caramel Sauce**, garnish dessert and serve.

THICKENING WITH STARCH

Starch is used to thicken and bind sauces. It is versatile, inexpensive and efficient in small amounts, and can be used without imparting a flavor of its own.

Starches must be combined with liquid and heated almost to a boiling point to be effective. When heated, the starch granules swell, allowing the starch to absorb up to 25 times their own weight. However, if a starch is overheated or exposed to heat for too long a period of time, it will hydrolyze, or breakdown, causing the sauce to thin out. If this happens to you, you can rescue your sauce by simply changing the starch! For example, if your sauce made with flour has broken, simply add a slurry (see the sidebar on p. 77) of corn-starch to rescue it.

Some starches are purer than others. Cornstarch, potato starch and arrow-root are almost pure starches, and produce shiny, clear sauces. They can be suitable for serving hot or cold depending on the dish.

In addition to starch, flour contains protein, which gives flour-thickened sauces a slightly mat appearance. Flour-based sauces are made with a roux, a blend of fat and flour cooked together. This serves two purposes: to coat the flour granules with fat as well as to cook them. Flour-based sauces are always served heated because the fat would be unpalatable if served at room temperature or chilled.

Baked Brie

Mouthwatering raspberries and rich, warm Brie…. The perfect hors d'oeurve to satisfy guests with a glass of cold, crisp Champagne, or a velvety Zinfandel or Syrah.

1 (14 to 15 inch) baguette, cut diagonally in ½ inch slices
2 – 3 tablespoons butter

1 (6 to 8 ounce) round of Brie
¼ cup brown sugar
1 tablespoon butter

¾ cup fresh or frozen raspberries
2 teaspoons sugar
1 teaspoon lemon juice
1 teaspoon corn starch
1 tablespoon sliced almonds

Butter baguette slices; place on cookie sheet and toast under broiler until golden. Set aside.

Preheat oven to 350°F. Place Brie in small ovenproof serving dish. Mound the brown sugar on top, dot with 1 tablespoon butter. Bake until the cheese is very soft, but not runny, about 15 minutes.

Meanwhile, in small saucepan, mix together raspberries, sugar, lemon juice and cornstarch. If you are using fresh raspberries, you may find it necessary to add 1 or 2 teaspoons water to cook them. Stir raspberry sauce over medium heat until boiling and slightly thickened, about 5 minutes. *This sauce can be prepared two days in advance. Refrigerate; reheat to serve.*

When cheese is done, remove from oven. Top with hot raspberry sauce; sprinkle with almonds. Serve immediately, surrounded with toasted baguette slices.

Serves 6 to 8.

Sautéed Prawns and Pineapple With Chili Oil Sauce

An appetizer I was served at a wonderful restaurant in the old city of Prague inspired the combination of flavors in this recipe. Your tastebuds will be teased by the combination of soy, ginger and hot chilies, and tantalized by the lightly caramelized pineapple and juicy shrimp.

For creme fraiche sauce:
6 tablespoons creme fraiche *(see sidebar)*, or sour cream
½ teaspoon freshly grated ginger
milk to thin, if necessary

For chili oil sauce:
2 tablespoons chili oil
1 clove garlic, minced
⅓ cup white wine
½ teaspoon freshly grated ginger
¼ cup soy sauce
2 tablespoons rice vinegar
1 teaspoon arrowroot
1 to 2 teaspoons sugar, to taste

2 tablespoons chili oil
24 tiger prawns *(about 1 pound)*, shelled and deveined, tails on
24 wedges of fresh pineapple *(about 4 ounces)*
1 spring onion, thinly sliced diagonally, for garnish

For sauce, stir ginger into creme fraiche or sour cream; thin with milk to consistency of syrup, set aside. Preheat a baking tray and your serving plates in a 160°F oven.

For chili oil sauce, heat 2 tablespoons chili oil in skillet over medium heat. Sauté garlic just until fragrant, add wine and ginger. Raise heat to high; reduce mixture to about 3 tablespoons. Meanwhile, stir together soy sauce, vinegar and arrowroot to form a slurry. Add slurry to reduced wine mixture; bring to a boil to thicken sauce slightly. Sprinkle sugar over sauce, adjust to taste. Remove from heat. Cover, keep warm.

Pat prawns dry with paper towel. Heat one tablespoon chili oil in sauté pan over high heat. Sauté prawns in hot oil just until opaque. Transfer to warmed tray in 160°F oven. Add remaining tablespoon chili oil to skillet. Cook pineapple until slightly browned. On preheated plates, arrange prawns on pineapple, drizzled with chili oil and ginger crème fraiche. Garnish with spring onion.

Serves 4 as a main dish.

Serve the prawns with julienne carrot bundles and Thai Jasmine rice (see the recipe in the sidebar on p. 139) to round out the meal. OR, cut the recipe in half, and serve as an elegant appetizer course!

EXTRA TOUCHES

CHILI OIL

½ cup vegetable oil
1 tablespoon dried chili flakes

In small saucepan, warm oil and chili flakes to about 160°F. (If you hold your hand above the oil, it should just feel warm.) Remove from heat. Pour into a sterile glass container; cover tightly. Shake jar or bottle every day for four days to redistribute the chilies.

Store in a cool, dark place. The chili oil will keep for about 4 months.

CREME FRAICHE

1 cup whipping cream, preferably organic
2 tablespoons cultured buttermilk

Stir together cream and buttermilk. Pour into a sterile glass jar; cover with a cloth. Set in a warm place (on top of the refrigerator is good) for 24 hours. Stir; the mixture should be slightly thickened and will continue to thicken when chilled. Refrigerate for up to two weeks.

JULIENNE CUTS

*When a recipe calls for food to be cut in **julienne**, or **julienne strips**, it simply means thin evenly sliced strips, like French fries, or the smaller version is often labeled "matchsticks."*

Slicing and cutting those round vegetables can be a challenge, but with a little skill and patience, the technique is easy.

To julienne-cut these carrots more easily, first cut a thin slice from one long side of the vegetable, creating a flat side. Now, rotate the carrot, placing the flat side down on your cutting surface for stability.

To make the julienne strips, continue cutting a thin slice from each of the three remaining long sides, creating a square-sided carrot. Now, slice lengthwise into thin slices. Stack the slices, and slice them lengthwise into julienne. Trim the ends to one size.

This technique of creating flat sides works well on most any oddly shaped fruit or vegetable!

Matchstick Carrot Bundles

3 medium carrots, washed, peeled and trimmed
1 teaspoon salt
4 long chives, about 7 – 8 inches in length each

Cut carrots into julienne strips, about ⅛ inch thick and wide, by 2½ inches in length, about the size of matchsticks. Divide into four even bundles.

In a wide shallow pan, bring a quart of water to a boil, add the salt. Add the chives to the boiling water; blanch for just a few seconds, then remove them from the water. Lay each chive out on a flat surface. Center a carrot bundle on each of the chives. Wrap the chive around the carrots and tie gently in a knot.

Lower the water temperature to simmer. Gently place the carrot bundles into the water, and cook 2 to 3 minutes, or until carrots are just softened. Remove from water, drain. *You can prepare to this point two days ahead. If preparing ahead, refresh carrot bundles in ice water after cooking. Remove when cooled, drain. Wrap cooked, cooled carrot bundles in plastic and refrigerate. To reheat, gently drop into simmering water for about 30 seconds, and serve immediately.*

Serves 4.

Banana Bread Pudding

My widowed grandmother ran a boarding house for many years where she served a wonderful, old-fashioned bread pudding. A more modern version baked in individual dishes and topped with caramel sauce, this comfort food becomes a sophisticated, upscale dessert.

2 eggs
1 cup whole milk or half-and-half
1 teaspoon almond extract
dash freshly grated nutmeg
6 cups Challah or Hawaiian-type bread, cut in ¾-inch dice
1 banana
2 tablespoons butter, plus a little for the dishes
¼ cup brown sugar
2 teaspoons Amaretto
¼ cup chocolate chips
1 tablespoon slivered almonds
2 teaspoons sugar, for tops
4 to 6 tablespoons Easy Caramel Sauce *(see sidebar)* or
    purchased caramel sauce
12 thin banana slices

Generously butter insides of four ramekins or custard cups; place on baking sheet, set aside. Preheat oven to 350°F.

Combine eggs, milk or half-and-half, vanilla and nutmeg. In large bowl, pour egg mixture over bread cubes, stir to mix well. Set aside for 15 minutes, stirring occasionally.

Meanwhile, quarter banana lengthwise, then cut into ¾-inch pieces. Melt butter in medium skillet over medium-high heat. Add banana pieces and brown sugar, cook until sugar is melted and bubbly. Remove from heat, stir in liqueur, and let cool.

Combine banana and egg mixtures, stir in chocolate chips. Spoon into prepared ramekins. *The recipe can be prepared to this point 4 to 5 hours in advance. Cover and refrigerate until ready to cook.*

Sprinkle tops of puddings with slivered almonds, then sugar. Bake in preheated oven 20 to 25 minutes. Tops should be golden brown and crunchy. Serve warm, drizzled with caramel sauce and garnished with banana slices.

Serves 4.

Variation: Add or substitute shredded coconut or your favorite chopped nuts with or in place of the chocolate chips.

EXTRA TOUCHES

EASY CARAMEL SAUCE

This is by far the easiest caramel sauce I have ever made. It is rich and smooth textured with a beautiful golden color.

Pour the contents of one 14-ounce can sweetened condensed milk into a 5 to 6 cup ovenproof dish with a lid. Cover tightly. Place the dish in a larger ovenproof dish. Pour water in the outer dish to a depth of 1½ inches.

Bake at 350°F for one to one and one half hours, stirring occasionally. Whisk to smooth consistency, if necessary. Cool. If desired, stir in 1 teaspoon vanilla extract or rum.

Store cooled caramel in a "squeezer" bottle in the refrigerator. Bring to room temperature to soften before use. The caramel will keep for 2 months.

Spring

Just the sound of the word gives me
energy. After the short, dark days of winter,
the pale greens, the purples and the bright
yellows of spring are exhilarating. It's time
to cook lighter fare. The markets offer
new spring asparagus, baby artichokes,
beautiful berries. And my herb garden is
beginning anew. Let the cooking reflect
your emotions and personality.

Chicken Picatta
Polenta
Green Bean Salad with Basil Vinaigrette

Tuscan Pears

Halibut with Tomatillo Cream Sauce
Mustard Potatoes
Mango, Cucumber and Jicama Salad

Oranges in Grand Marnier

Fettucini with Asparagus & Cream
Orange & Lemon Salad

Champagne Zabaglione with Fresh Peaches

Pan-Seared Salmon with Black Bean Salsa

Chocolate Raspberry Truffle Torte

Spring Menus

EPHEMERAL PRIMAVERA

Sun-Dried Tomato Pesto Crostini

Chicken Picatta

Polenta

Green Bean Salad with Basil Vinaigrette

Tuscan Pears

FIRST BUDS OF SPRING

Artichoke and Lemon Cheese Spread

Halibut with Tomatillo Cream

Mustard Potatoes

Mango, Cucumber and Jicama Salad

Oranges in Grand Mariner

SIMPLE SPRINGTIDE SUPPER

New Potatoes with Olive Pesto

Fettuccini with Asparagus and Cream

Orange and Lemon Salad

Champagne Zabaglione with Fresh Fruit

A CELEBRATION OF NEW BEGINNINGS

Greek Lemon Soup

Pan-Seared Salmon with Black Bean Salsa

Make Ahead Rice

Rouille

Chocolate Raspberry Truffle Torte

Ephemeral Primavera

Sun-Dried Tomato Pesto Crostini

◆

Chicken Picatta

Polenta

Green Bean Salad
with
Basil Vinaigrette

Breads
(purchased)

*Trebbiano or
Sangiovese*

◆

Tuscan Pears

◆

Coffee and Tea

Ephemeral Primavera

Three days ahead:
Prepare **Sun-Dried Tomato Pesto**. Refrigerate.
Wash, trim and steam beans for **Green Bean Salad with Basil Vinaigrette**.
Fold the napkins if desired.

Two days ahead:
Cook **Polenta**, adding optional seasonings if desired. Spread in dampened pan, cover and refrigerate.

The day before:
Toast the pine nuts for **Tuscan Pears**. Cover and set aside
Put butter on its serving plate or bowl, cover and refrigerate.
Chill the wine and other cold beverages.
Set up coffee or tea tray, after dinner drinks, glasses, etc.
Make ice.
Set the table. Put out any non-food items (salt and pepper, wine coaster, etc.)
Arrange the flowers.

The morning before:
Cut **Polenta** into serving pieces, arrange on baking sheet, brush with oil. Cover and refrigerate.
Set up coffee maker.

6 hours before guests arrive:
Split chicken breasts and flour for **Chicken Picatta**.
Slice bread, spread with olive oil and place on baking sheet for **Sun-Dried Tomato Pesto Crostini**. Cover with plastic wrap.

1 – 2 hours before guests arrive:
Prepare vinaigrette for **Green Bean Salad with Basil Vinaigrette**. Set aside.
Remove butter from refrigerator to soften.
Slice purchased bread, if serving.

Before your guests arrive:
Preheat broiler for crostini. Toast bread slices, top with pesto for **Sun-Dried Tomato Crostini**. Arrange on platter.
Broil **Polenta** until golden; hold in preheated oven.
Preheat oven to 160° F for **Chicken Picatta**. Sauté chicken breasts; hold in preheated oven. Prepare sauce, cover and
    remove from heat.
Toss beans with dressing for **Green Bean Salad with Basil Vinaigrette**. Divide onto serving plates, garnish and place on
    serving table.
Preheat the plates and platters as needed.

After the guests arrive:
Reheat the lemon sauce for the **Chicken Picatta**; serve on warmed plates with the **Polenta**.
Slice the pears for **Tuscan Pears**. Drizzle with oil; finish with thyme and cheese. Serve at room temperature.

EXTRA TOUCHES

SUN-DRIED TOMATOES

If you have a bumper crop of tomatoes, you can easily make your own sun-dried tomatoes. Serve as garnish, in salads, sauces, or make tomato pesto as in the recipe at right.

For sun-dried tomatoes:

small Roma or cherry tomatoes
coarse salt (I use Margarita salt)
vinegar
olive oil
fresh rosemary, basil, or thyme
*   leaves (optional)*

Cut Roma tomatoes into quarters or cherry tomatoes into halves. Arrange the tomato pieces cut-side up on a baking sheet. Sprinkle with salt. Place the baking sheet in a preheated 200°F oven for about 7 hours. Watch tomatoes carefully to make sure they do not burn, checking every half hour after the first four hours of cooking.

When pieces dry completely, they should have a dried, shriveled appearance, feeling dry to the touch, but still soft like a raisin. As individual pieces dry completely, remove from the oven; let cool.

To store refrigerated: Dip each dried tomato in vinegar, and layer in a sterile glass jar. Cover the tomatoes completely with olive oil. Add optional herbs if desired. DO NOT ADD GARLIC to avoid danger of botulism contamination. These tomatoes will last for months.

To store frozen: Place cooled dried tomatoes in heavy plastic freezer bag, seal tightly. Store in freezer, will keep 6 months.

One pound of tomatoes yields about two ounces sun-dried. No wonder they are SO EXPENSIVE!

Sun-Dried Tomato Pesto Crostini

A tasteful and colorful year-round appetizer or snack. that is quickly prepared if you have a store of sun-dried tomatoes in your refrigerator, freezer or pantry.

½ cup red wine vinegar
1 cup sun-dried tomatoes
2 cloves garlic, minced
olive oil (possibly drained from the tomatoes)
½ teaspoon freshly grated lemon zest
½ teaspoon thyme
salt and pepper to taste

small slices of coarse Italian bread
olive oil

For the pesto:
Heat vinegar to a boil. Pour over tomatoes; let stand 10 to 15 minutes to rehydrate. Drain off any excess vinegar and reserve. To make this recipe by hand: Chop tomatoes finely, combine with the minced garlic. Add olive oil a little at a time until desired spreading consistency is reached. Add zest, thyme, salt and pepper to taste.

If you have a food processor: With the machine running, add peeled garlic cloves. When garlic is minced, add tomatoes, zest and thyme. Process until finely chopped. Add olive oil bit by bit until desired consistency is reached. Salt and pepper to taste.

The pesto may be made a week in advance. Refrigerate to store. Makes 1 cup pesto.

For the crostini:
Preheat the broiler. Spread the bread slices with a bit of olive oil. Toast under the broiler until lightly browned. Top with a little of the tomato spread. Serve immediately.

Chicken Picatta

Tangy, fresh lemon and caper sauce surrounding fork tender chicken breasts, a popular Italian classic that is destined to become a favorite with family and guests alike. This is one of my favorite recipes for entertaining because I can do so much of the preparation in advance, and it is so easy!

4 boneless, skinless chicken breasts (*4 ounces each*)
½ cup flour
salt and pepper
3 tablespoons butter, *divided*
1 tablespoon olive oil
2 – 3 cloves garlic, minced
1 cup plus 2 tablespoons dry white wine, *divided*
(I recommend Trebbiano** for the most authentic flavor)
1½ teaspoon cornstarch
1 cup chicken stock or broth
2 teaspoons freshly grated lemon zest
1 teaspoon fresh lemon juice
2 tablespoons capers, drained
salt and pepper to taste
1 tablespoon freshly minced parsley
4 thin lemon slices, for garnish

Preheat oven and baking sheet to 160°F. With a sharp knife, split each chicken breast horizontally into two thin cutlets. Dredge each cutlet in flour seasoned with salt and pepper. (*This can be done up to six hours ahead, cover and refrigerate.*)

In a large non-reactive skillet (*see sidebar on p. 55*), heat 1 tablespoon of the butter and the olive oil over medium high heat. Add the chicken breasts in a single layer, do not crowd. You may need to cook the breasts in batches. Cook two minutes on each side, until golden brown. Transfer breasts to heated baking sheet, keep warm.

In a small bowl combine 2 tablespoons of the wine with the cornstarch; set aside. Add one tablespoon of the butter to the skillet, sauté the garlic just until fragrant. Pour in the remaining wine, stock, lemon zest and juice. Stir, scraping up any browned bits of chicken from the pan to flavor the sauce. Reduce over high heat to about ¾ cup. Add the wine and cornstarch slurry; bring the mixture to a boil to thicken slightly. Remove the sauce from the heat, and stir in the remaining 2 tablespoons butter and the capers. Check the seasoning. To serve cutlets: top with sauce, sprinkle with parsley, and garnish each with a lemon slice.

Serves 4.

**If you are unable to find Trebbiano wine, Gewürztraminer is an acceptable substitute.*

COOKING CLASS

SAUTÉING

Sautéing is an important method of cooking foods, easily mastered for perfection every time. Simply described, it is cooking food quickly over high heat in a small amount of fat, to achieve a nice golden brown result. You just need to know the rules:

1. The food must be **dry**. Wet food creates steam and doesn't brown well.

2. The food must be **at room temperature** to cook properly all the way through. Allow 15 minutes out of the refrigerator to accomplish this.

3. The pan must be **hot** when the food is added.

4. Either the food or the pan must be coated with some type of **fat** to promote browning.

5. **Do not crowd** the food in the pan. Air circulation prevents steam from forming, and allows for more even cooking.

6. When sautéing, you should **turn the food every two minutes** until done, to promote even cooking and to prevent burning.

7. **Do not cover** the food during the cooking process, as this creates steam.

Once this technique has been mastered, it can be used successfully to cook all kinds of foods well.

Polenta is a type of cornmeal, which is a staple in Northern Italian cuisine. It can be served as a first course, as a side dish for an entrée, or as a hearty breakfast with a little brown sugar, nutmeg and cinnamon added. For breakfast, the polenta would be spooned right out of the pot into a breakfast bowl. With main meals, polenta may be served straight from the pot, or it may be allowed to set up in a mold, sliced, and browned on a grill or sautéed. It is a lovely accompaniment.

Coarse-ground polenta is preferable if you can find it because of its superior flavor and texture, but medium-ground cornmeal will work.

There are two grinding styles for polenta: steel-ground or stone/water-ground. The steel grinding method removes most of the husk and the germ, extending the shelf life almost indefinitely if stored in an airtight container. The stone/water grinding method leaves most of the germ and husk, making the meal more nutritious, but it is more perishable because of the fat from the germ. It should be stored in an airtight container in the refrigerator, for up to 4 months.

You will find coarse-ground polenta at specialty markets, or larger supermarkets.

Polenta

I discovered polenta during my first stay in Italy. I immediately fell in love with the crunchy and golden crust, smooth and creamy inside. An unusual but simple side dish classically served with Italian meals, another Italian comfort food.

2 cups chicken or vegetable stock or broth
½ cup coarse-ground polenta, or medium-ground cornmeal
salt to taste

2 tablespoons olive oil or butter, for broiling

Optional seasonings:
    1 – 2 tablespoons freshly snipped chives and
    3 tablespoons freshly grated Parmesan cheese or
    3 – 4 tablespoons crumbled blue cheese
or
    3 tablespoons chopped, roasted red peppers
    ½ cup cooked crumbled sausage, drained

In large saucepan, heat stock to boiling; lower heat. Slowly pour in cornmeal, stirring constantly to prevent lumps. Return to boil; lower heat slightly. Stir and cook about 15 minutes for regular-ground cornmeal, or as long as 40 minutes for coarse-ground polenta, until the grains are very soft and no longer taste "raw." *If the constant stirring is a problem, cook the polenta over a double boiler (see sidebar on p. 135). It will take a bit longer, but will require only occasional stirring.*

When the polenta is done, stir in the seasonings of your choice. Pour immediately into a dampened 8-inch square pan. Let cool until just warm to the touch. *You may make the polenta to this point up to two days in advance; cover and chill until ready to continue.*

Preheat the broiler. Turn cooled polenta out of pan onto cutting board. Cut into circles or triangles. Arrange on a greased baking sheet. Brush with butter or olive oil. Broil until golden on each side. Transfer to warm plate in 160°F oven if necessary to hold, until serving.

Serves 4.

Green Bean Salad
With Basil Vinaigrette

Tender-crisp beans surrounded with the tangy zip of vinaigrette and the appealing aroma of fresh basil.

1 pound green beans, washed and trimmed
1 tablespoon balsamic or red wine vinegar
¼ teaspoon Dijon mustard
¼ teaspoon salt
freshly ground pepper
¼ cup Extra-virgin olive oil
2 shallots, minced
8 – 12 fresh basil leaves, cut in chiffonade *(see sidebar on p. 39)*
2 tablespoons freshly grated Romano or Parmesan cheese

Cook beans in boiling salted water until just tender crisp and bright green. Remove beans from boiling water and refresh in cold water for 3 to 4 minutes. When cooled, drain the beans well; set side to dry. *The beans can be prepared ahead to this point, wrapped in a paper towel and plastic wrap and refrigerated up to three days.*

Combine vinegar, mustard, salt and pepper; whisk to dissolve salt. Continue whisking constantly; gradually add oil to create an emulsion. When all of the oil has been incorporated, stir in shallots and basil leaves, reserving a bit of the basil for garnish. *You can prepare the dressing as much as two hours in advance and store at room temperature until use.*

Toss beans with about half of the dressing, and arrange on a platter. Top with remaining dressing. Sprinkle with cheese and reserved basil.

Serves 4.

COOKING CLASS

VINAIGRETTES

Freshly made vinaigrette dressings highlight any salad or vegetable, and can even be used as great marinades. The technique is easily mastered by hand, as well as in a blender or food processor.

First combine the acid (usually vinegar or lemon juice) with the salt, pepper and mustard. Mustard is added as an emulsifier, to prevent the dressing from separating. Whisk by hand or process in a food processor or blender until the salt is dissolved. Continue whisking constantly, or with the machine running, and begin to add the oil a few drops at a time. When about one tablespoon of the oil has been incorporated and there are no visible streaks of oil floating on top of the dressing, you may begin to add the remaining oil in a slow, steady stream. It is imperative for the oil to be added gradually, or the emulsion process will not occur, and you will be left with oil floating on vinegar. As the last third of the oil is added, the mixture should thicken slightly.

Vinaigrette can be stored for a few hours at room temperature, but may separate if refrigerated. Should this happen, you might try rewhisking the mixture, but it will most likely separate again very quickly.

To slice pears quickly and easily for this recipe, use a chef's tip: cut one side of the pear away from the core, repeat with the other side.

Then simply cut away the small portions left on either side of the core.

To slice the pear thinly, stabilize the fruit by placing the flat edges down on your cutting surface, the rounded sides facing up. Slice.

This technique works well with apples too.

Tuscan Pears

This beautiful, fresh but not too sweet salad recipe was inspired by Chef Judy Witts, who taught me to cook Tuscan food in Florence, Italy. You will be happiest with fresh thyme and the best quality imported Parmesan cheese available for these pears. This salad can also double as a light dessert, in the European style of a cheese course.

2 tablespoons pine nuts
4 ripe pears, cored and thinly sliced
1 – 2 tablespoons best quality olive oil
1 – 2 teaspoons thyme
slivered Parmesan cheese

Toast pine nuts in skillet over medium heat until golden brown. Set aside to cool. Arrange pears on serving plate. Drizzle with olive oil and sprinkle with thyme. Top with the toasted pine nuts and the slivers of Parmesan.

Serves 4.

First Buds of Spring

Artichoke and Lemon Cheese Spread
With Crackers

◆

Halibut with Tomatillo Cream

Mustard Potatoes

Mango, Cucumber and Jicama Salad

Breads
(purchased)

◆

Pinot Noir

◆

Oranges in Grand Marnier

◆

Coffee and Tea

First Buds of Spring

Three days ahead:
Prepare **Artichoke and Lemon Cheese Spread**. Divide into two crocks, reserving one for another use.
Prepare simple syrup for **Oranges in Grand Marnier**.
Fold the napkins if desired.

The day before:
Shop for fish for **Halibut with Tomatillo Cream**.
Put butter on its serving plate or bowl, cover and refrigerate.
Chill the wine and other cold beverages.
Set up coffee or tea tray, after dinner drinks, glasses, etc.
Make ice.
Set the table. Put out any non-food items (salt and pepper, wine coaster, etc.)
Arrange the flowers.

The morning before:
Finish preparation of **Oranges in Grand Marnier**.
Cut vegetables and fruit for **Mango, Cucumber and Jicama Salad**. If space allows, refrigerate arranged on serving plates.
Line baking sheet with parchment for **Mustard Potatoes**. Scrub potatoes, let dry.
Set up coffee maker.

6 hours before guests arrive:
Prepare mustard mixture for **Mustard Potatoes**.

1 – 2 hours before guests arrive:
Prepare **Tomatillo Cream Sauce**; cover and set aside.
Dress **Mango, Cucumber and Jicama Salad** with lime and chili powder. Garnish with cilantro. Chill until serving time.
Remove butter from refrigerator to soften.
Slice purchased bread, if serving.

Before your guests arrive:
Arrange cheese crock and crackers on serving plate.
Preheat the oven for **Halibut with Tomatillo Cream Sauce**.
Toss potatoes with mustard mixture for **Mustard Potatoes**, spread on prepared baking sheet.
Divide **Oranges in Grand Marnier** into serving bowls or goblets. Garnish as desired. Set aside.
Preheat the plates and platters as needed.

After the guests arrive: Allow halibut to stand 15 minutes to come to room temperature before cooking. Reheat **Tomatillo Cream Sauce**. Cook halibut according to recipe, serve on warmed plates.
Roast **Mustard Potatoes** according to recipe.

Artichoke and Lemon Cheese Spread

A luscious yet light lemony spread, easily prepared by hand or in a food processor.

1 clove garlic
1 small jar (6.5 ounces) marinated artichoke hearts, drained
freshly grated zest of ½ lemon
1 teaspoon freshly squeezed lemon juice
½ teaspoon dried thyme
1 (8 ounce) package cream cheese, softened
salt and pepper to taste

Food processor method:

Drop garlic through feed tube with machine running to mince. Add artichoke hearts; pulse-process to chop. Add lemon zest and juice, thyme and cream cheese. Process to blend. Correct seasonings.

By hand:

Mince garlic. Chop artichoke hearts finely. Combine garlic, artichoke hearts, lemon zest and juice, thyme and cream cheese in mixing bowl. Blend well. Correct seasonings.

To serve:

Spoon cheese mixture into two 6-ounce crocks or ramekins, smoothing the tops. Cover tightly and chill. *Make ahead and refrigerate up to one week, or freeze for two months.*

Let stand at room temperature 10 to 15 minutes before serving to soften. Serve on a tray surrounded with crackers or small toasts, or with a pastry bag, pipe rosettes of the cheese spread onto crackers for a more elegant presentation. Sprinkle with freshly chopped chives.

Makes two crocks, each serving four.

TIMESAVER!

SOFTENING CREAM CHEESE

To soften cream cheese quickly, unwrap it and place in a microwave safe bowl. Microwave at 50% power for 1 minute. Let stand 1 minute before using.

Halibut with Tomatillo Cream

The light, delicate nature of halibut is complimented beautifully with the spicy sophisticated cream sauce. It will become a habit.

1 tablespoon olive oil
1 shallot, minced
1 clove garlic, minced
dash of salt
½ cup dry white wine
½ cup Mexican Salsa Verde (about ½ can)
2 tablespoons chopped canned green chiles
1 chicken bouillon cube
½ cup whipping cream

1 – 2 tablespoons olive or vegetable oil
1¼ pounds halibut fillet**, cut into 4 portions
salt and pepper to taste

Preheat oven to 450°F. Place a baking sheet in oven to preheat.

In small skillet, heat oil over high heat. Sauté shallot and garlic with salt until fragrant but not browned, about 2 minutes. Add wine; reduce mixture to 2 tablespoons. Add salsa verde, chilies, bouillon cube and cream; stir to combine. Bring to a boil; cook 3 to 4 minutes longer, until sauce coats the back of a spoon. Set aside, cover and keep warm. *The sauce can be prepared 1 hour ahead. Reheat to serve.*

In large skillet, heat olive oil over medium high heat. Dry fish fillets with paper towel before cooking. Season with salt and pepper. Gently place fish in hot pan, cook 2 to 3 minutes per side, until just beginning to turn golden.

Transfer fish to heated baking sheet, place in oven. Roast 4 to 6 minutes. Internal temperature should reach 135°F. Remove fish from oven, let stand 4 minutes longer. Internal temperature should then be 145°F. Serve on heated plates, topped with sauce.

Serves 4.

**If halibut is not available, you may want to substitute cod or salmon.*

KNOW YOUR INGREDIENTS

SALSA VERDE

Salsa verde is a canned product from Mexico. It is made from tomatillos, chilies, onions, garlic and spices. Tomatillos are small green vegetables with a golden papery husk. They resemble small tomatoes, but tend to be more acidic, not quite as sweet. You will find salsa verde in the ethnic section of your supermarket or at a Mexican specialty shop.

GREEN CHILES

Green chiles are a canned product, found in your supermarket's ethnic section. They are mild California chiles that have been roasted and peeled, then canned.

I always have leftover salsa verde and chopped green chiles after preparing this recipe. I simply put them in labeled, zip-top plastic freezer bags, squeezing out excess air. Then I flatten the bags and freeze. They will keep 6 months in the freezer.

KNOW YOUR INGREDIENTS

POTATOES

In the United States we cultivate the following common varieties of potatoes:

Russet or Idaho potatoes are long, with a thicker brown rough skin. They have a low moisture and high starch content, making them ideal for baking.

Long whites or white roses have thinner skin and much smaller eyes. They are suitable for baking, roasting or boiling.

Round white potatoes have a brown skin, vs. the **round red, which** has a reddish skin. Low in starch and high in moisture with waxy flesh, both are ideal for boiling, frying and roasting.

Yukon gold and **Finnish yellow** potatoes have recently become quite popular. They are distinguished by their yellow flesh. They make beautiful mashed potatoes.

New potatoes are not one particular variety; they are just young potatoes harvested early in the season.

Regardless of variety, chose potatoes free of sprouts, cracks, wrinkles, decay or green areas. Buy only as many as you will use within two weeks.

Store the potatoes in a cool place, around 50°F with plenty of ventilation — not in a plastic bag.

Mustard Potatoes

Inspired by the beautiful mustard fields and myriad of mustards available in Napa Valley, I created these golden, sizzling and savory potatoes as a surprising accompaniment.

1½ pounds small new potatoes, scrubbed, dried
1 tablespoon olive oil
2 tablespoons country style whole grain mustard
1 clove garlic, minced
¾ teaspoon salt
¼ teaspoon freshly ground black pepper
2 – 3 tablespoons Italian parsley, snipped

Preheat oven to 450°F. Line a large baking sheet with parchment paper. If necessary, halve or quarter any potatoes that are larger than "bite size." All of the potatoes or pieces should be about the same size, to ensure even cooking.

In a large bowl, combine olive oil, mustard, garlic, salt and pepper. *You may prepare this recipe to this point 4 to 5 hours in advance.*

Add potatoes to mustard mixture, toss to coat. Spread potatoes on parchment lined sheet. Roast potatoes in preheated oven 20 to 35 minutes depending on the size of the potatoes. The potatoes should be soft in the center. Serve hot sprinkled with parsley.

Serves 4.

Mango, Cucumber and Jicama Salad

A beautiful and cool accompaniment, presenting a variety of textures and showcasing the fresh ingredients of our southern neighbor.

1 large mango, thinly sliced *(see sidebar at left)*
½ large cucumber, peeled, seeded if desired, thinly sliced
½ medium jicama**, peeled, and cut into julienne strips
    or about 6 radishes, trimmed and cut into julienne strips
freshly squeezed juice of ½ lime
chili powder, for garnish
cilantro, for garnish

Arrange mango slices, cucumber slices and jicama or radish strips on serving platter. Sprinkle with lime juice, then with chili powder. Garnish with cilantro. Serve immediately, or prepare in advance up to four hours. Refrigerate to store.

Serves 4.

****Jicama,** *(pronounced HEE-kah-mah), is a root vegetable native to Mexico, with a light brown skin and a white interior. It is favored for its wonderful crisp texture, like a water chestnut, and its slightly sweet, nutty flavor. You can find it at Mexican markets or most large supermarkets. Store it refrigerated. Peel it just before using.*

To peel jicama, use a sharp knife to pull away the brown skin in sheets.

TECHNIQUE

Slicing and peeling mangoes *are easy tasks, if you have a bit of skill. First, stand the mango on its end. Remove the pit by cutting a slice off either flat side, leaving a center slice about 1 inch thick. That is the pit. Discard it.*

Then, carefully cut thin slices into the flesh of the mango, down to but not through the skin.

Finally, run the knife around the sides next to the skin, releasing the fruit slices.

BLOOD ORANGES

There are so many varieties of oranges in the market; it is helpful to know which varieties will work best in this recipe. I like to use Navel oranges because of their large size, shape and bright color. An added benefit is that there are no seeds that must be removed. And when available, I use blood oranges.

Blood oranges most often come from Italy, but are now being raised in the U.S. and can be found in gourmet markets and some farmers' markets.

They are not always recognizable. The skin is sometimes tinged with a blush, but most often, they appear to be just like any other orange on the outside. Don't be fooled. On the inside, they have spots of red, varying from orangey-red to ruby. They are very sweet and fresh tasting, providing a unique color to this healthy and very flavorful dessert.

I will never forget my first introduction to blood oranges. I had purchased what I thought were regular oranges in the market. Upon slicing one in half to serve it, I saw the bright red interior, and thought something was terribly wrong with the orange. So, I threw it away — now I know better!

Oranges in Grand Marnier

This dessert always brings back the wonderful memory of my family's favorite eating spot in London, Ristorante Ana Capri. We are always treated like family there in the true Neapolitan tradition, and the food was always exquisite.

4 large Navel oranges (some blood oranges, if available)
⅓ cup Simple syrup*
4 tablespoons Grand Marnier

4 tablespoons Mascarpone cheese,** optional
mint sprigs, for garnish

Zest two of the oranges, reserving the zest. Then, using a very sharp knife, peel all four of the oranges, taking care to remove all of the white pith. This is more easily accomplished by slicing off the ends of the orange, then standing it on its cut end. Remove the peel from the side by cutting down in strips, moving around the orange, until all of the peel has been removed.

Either slice the oranges crosswise into wheels, or slice into supremes *(see sidebar on p. 34)*, taking care to catch any juices. Remove as many seeds as possible.

Place oranges in large bowl. Pour simple syrup and Grand Marnier over oranges, add grated zest, and stir. Cover and set aside to marinate, at least one hour. Serve garnished with a dollop of Mascarpone cheese and a sprig of mint if desired.

Serves 4.

Simple syrup:
¼ cup sugar
¼ cup water

Bring to boil, cool. Makes about ⅓ cup. Refrigerate to store. The syrup should keep approximately three weeks.

**Mascarpone cheese is Italian cream cheese, a very rich, creamy textured soft cheese available in gourmet supermarkets and Italian markets.

Simple Springtide Supper

New Potatoes with Olive Pesto

◆

Fettuccini
with
Asparagus and Cream

Orange and Lemon
Salad

Breads
(purchased)

*Pinot Gris or
Sauvignon Blanc
(served very cold)*

◆

Champagne Zabaglione
with
Fresh Fruit

◆

Coffee and Tea

Simple Springtide Supper

Three days ahead:
Prepare pesto for **New Potatoes with Olive Pesto**. Chill.
Fold the napkins if desired.

Two days ahead:
Shop for fresh asparagus and fruit
Cook potatoes for **New Potatoes with Olive Pesto**. Cover and refrigerate.

The day before:
Wash and trim asparagus for **Fettuccini with Asparagus and Cream**. Cut asparagus according to recipe; wrap
and refrigerate.
Prepare **Champagne Zabaglione**. Cover tightly and chill.
Put butter on its serving plate or bowl, cover and refrigerate.
Chill the wine and other cold beverages.
Set up coffee or tea tray, after dinner drinks, glasses, etc.
Make ice.
Set the table. Put out any non-food items (salt and pepper, wine coaster, etc.)
Arrange the flowers.

The morning before:
Cut fresh fruit for **Champagne Zabaglione with Fresh Fruit**. If space allows, refrigerate in serving dishes.
Set up coffee maker.

3 hours before guests arrive:
Prepare **Orange and Lemon Salad**. Set aside.

1   2 hours before guests arrive:
Prepare sauce for **Fettuccini with Asparagus and Cream**.
Remove butter from refrigerator to soften.
Slice purchased bread, if serving.

Before your guests arrive:
Heat large pot of water for **Fettuccini with Asparagus and Cream**. Grate Parmesan .
Halve potatoes, top with pesto and garnish. Arrange the **New Potatoes with Olive Pesto** on serving platter.
Arrange fruit in serving dishes for dessert, if necessary.
Preheat the plates and platters as needed.

After the guests arrive:
Cook pasta and reheat sauce for **Fettuccini with Asparagus and Cream**.
Spoon **Champagne Zabaglione** over plated fruit, garnish and serve.

More than ninety percent of the world's olives are produced near the Mediterranean. Olives imported from this region are known for their superior flavor and texture.

Purplish-black Kalamata olives come from Greece, and are characterized by the bite of the vinegar in which they have been cured.

The tiny, brown Niçoise olives from France are first cured in brine, then packed in olive oil.

Provençal olives also from France are medium green, marinated in olive oil with herbs.

The small round reddish-brown Gaeta olives from southern Italy are cured in brine, then packed in olive oil. You will find them slightly bitter.

Manzanilla olives from Spain are medium-size, pale green and slightly sweeter than other olives.

These are but a few of the hundreds of olive varieties available in the marketplace. Wonderfully flavorful olives are also produced in South America, Northern Africa, and much closer to home, in our own California!

New Potatoes with Olive Pesto

This pesto is also a great spread for crackers or crostini, as well as a lovely filling for stuffing mushrooms or cherry tomatoes.

½ pound new potatoes, scrubbed
1 teaspoon salt
½ cup black and green olives, preferably imported
1 shallot
1 clove garlic
1 tablespoon capers
1 teaspoon anchovy paste
1 teaspoon basil
1 teaspoon oregano
1 teaspoon rosemary
2 tablespoons Extra-virgin olive oil
½ teaspoon balsamic vinegar, or red wine vinegar, or lemon juice
fresh parsley, for garnish

Place potatoes in saucepan; cover with cold water. Bring to boil over high heat, add salt. Reduce heat to simmer; only a few bubbles should appear. Cook potatoes until easily pierced with a knife, 20 to 25 minutes. Drain. Cover potatoes with cold water; let stand 5 minutes, then drain again. Pat potatoes dry. *Potatoes can be prepared to this point up to 2 days in advance. Cover and refrigerate until ready to use.*

To prepare the pesto, pit olives, if necessary *(see sidebar on p. 16)*. Combine all ingredients in food processor and process just until mixed, but not smooth. *Can be refrigerated up to 3 weeks.*

Makes about ½ cup.

To serve: Cut potatoes in half lengthwise. Spread the cut surface of each potato half generously with the olive pesto. Garnish with a fresh parsley leaf. Arrange the potato halves on a tray. Serve at room temperature.

Makes about 16 appetizers.

Fettuccini with Asparagus and Cream

1 pound asparagus, trimmed
2 tablespoons unsalted butter
¾ cup heavy cream
8 ounces fettuccini
¼ cup freshly grated Parmesan (best quality possible)
3 – 4 grinds of freshly ground nutmeg
salt
ground white pepper

Cut off asparagus tips, and reserve. Cut the stalks into ¼-inch diagonal slices. *This may be done up to one day in advance. Wrap tips and slices separately and refrigerate.*

To continue: in large skillet, melt butter over medium heat, add sliced asparagus. Cook 2 to 3 minutes, shaking pan occasionally. Asparagus should be slightly tender and bright green. Raise heat to medium-high, add cream and asparagus tips. Boil until sauce is slightly reduced and lightly thickened, 4 to 5 minutes. *You can put the sauce on hold here if necessary. Remove from heat and cover. Gently reheat if necessary.*

Cook fettuccini according to manufacturer's directions. Drain. When pasta is done and drained, add to the cream sauce. Add a little of the hot pasta water if necessary to thin the sauce. Toss with Parmesan, nutmeg, salt and pepper. Serve hot.

Makes 4 servings.

KNOW YOUR INGREDIENTS

ASPARAGUS

Asparagus should have mild, sweet taste and a crisp-tender texture. Choose the thick or thin spears, according to your own preference. Thin stalks are more tender than thicker, but can be accommodated by peeling the thicker stalks, see below. Look for spears of uniform size, so all stalks will cook in the same amount of time. Select straight, firm, green stalks with tightly closed tips. To store the asparagus, stand it in about two inches of water and cover loosely, refrigerate. It should be used within 24 hours. Local asparagus is usually available from mid-April through June, California asparagus has extended the period of availability.

To prepare the asparagus, wash the spears, bend each spear gently. It will snap at the point where tenderness begins. Reserve the woody stem ends for another use, such as in soups, salads, purees, or as finger food. Peeling is optional.

At only 35 calories per cup of cooked asparagus, it is a very healthy choice. It is also an excellent source of Vitamins C and A, as well as iron.

TECHNIQUE

PEELING ASPARAGUS

The "woody" texture of thick asparagus spears can be tamed by peeling, but the task can be daunting. Here's a quick chef's tip: rest the spear on a cutting board. Holding the spear by the tip, use a peeler. Scrape away the thin outer layer beginning about an inch below the tips all the way to the base of the spear.

Orange and Lemon Salad

This classic Italian salad always reminds me of warm, sunny spring days in southern Italy, from where it originates. The first time you try it, you will agree that the unlikely matching of flavors produces a vibrant, lively and always beautiful side dish.

4 oranges (*blood oranges if you can find them; see sidebar on p. 128*)
1 or 2 lemons, very ripe (*Meyer lemons if you can find them; see sidebar on p. 25*)
1 small red onion
6 fresh basil leaves, or fresh mint, or combination of both
freshly ground black pepper
4 teaspoons Extra-Virgin olive oil

With a very sharp knife, peel oranges and lemons, removing all the white pith *(see sidebar on p. 34 for peeling instructions)*. Slice oranges into medium slices, lemons somewhat thinner. Remove any visible seeds.

Layer overlapping orange and lemon slices on a serving platter or on individual plates. Thinly slice or chop the onion, arrange over fruit slices. Cut large basil or mint leaves in chiffonade *(see sidebar on p. 39)*. Small leaves may remain whole. Scatter leaves over the fruit. Sprinkle generously with black pepper, and drizzle with olive oil.

Let stand one to three hours before serving. The salad should be served at room temperature.

Serves 4.

COOKING CLASS

You may have noticed a number of Italian salad and vegetable dishes in this book, all of which may be served at room temperature. This is the classic presentation of most side dishes from that region.

As refrigerators in Europe are much smaller than our American counterparts, cold space is at a premium. Many fruit and vegetable dishes with high acid content are prepared ahead, covered and left at room temperature until serving time. The high acid content prevents pathogen growth.

Champagne Zabaglione With Fresh Fruit

Pronounced zah-ball-YO-nay (the "G" is silent), this is the Italian equivalent of French Sabayon, or egg custard sauce. Zabaglione is traditionally prepared using Marsala wine. This version is much lighter in both texture and color, pairing nicely with fresh fruits like berries, peaches or oranges.

2 egg yolks
2 tablespoons sugar
pinch of salt
pinch of cinnamon
⅓ cup dry Champagne

2 cups fresh fruit, peeled and cut bite-size if necessary
⅓ cup dry Champagne (optional)

Over simmering water, beat yolks, sugar, salt and cinnamon in top of double boiler until lemon-colored and ribbon trail forms when beater is lifted *(see sidebar on p. 79)*.

Add one-third of the Champagne, beat until foamy. Repeat until all Champagne is incorporated into egg mixture. Beat until mixture mounds on spoon. Chill. *Zabaglione may be prepared one day in advance and chilled until ready to serve.*

Toss fruit with Champagne if desired to prevent browning. Divide into serving dishes or on plates. Spoon chilled zabaglione atop sliced fruit to serve. Garnish with fresh mint.

Makes 4 servings.

Variation: Substitute an unoaked Chardonnay (Australian varieties are nice) for the Champagne. Or for traditional Zabaglione, use Marsala in place of the Champagne, omit cinnamon.

THE RIGHT TOOLS

DOUBLE BOILER

Also known as a "Bain Marie," a double boiler is used to gently heat delicate foods, or to keep foods warm.

There is only one rule: the water should barely simmer but not boil. Most likely, the food you are heating is not to rise above 160°F, so the water must not be much hotter than that.

You don't have to have a special type of pan to create your own double boiler. A deep wide skillet will work very well. Fill the pan with water to a depth of 1 to 1½ inches. Lay a paper towel on the bottom of the pan. The towel acts as an insulator while allowing some water to flow under the bowl above, and preventing scratching your pan.

Place the skillet over low heat, adjusting the heat as necessary to maintain the proper temperature.

Use a metal bowl to hold the food you are heating. Simply place it in the hot water bath, and cook as directed.

The advantage of this method is that you can see instantly if the water becomes too hot and begins to boil or if the water level becomes too low.

A Celebration of New Beginnings

Greek Lemon Soup

Sauvignon Blanc

◆

Pan-Seared
Salmon
with
Black Bean Salsa

Make Ahead Rice

Rouille

Assorted Breads
(purchased)
Flavored Butter
(optional, see recipes in
"Show-Offs!!" section)

*Pinot Gris or
Pinot Noir*

◆

Chocolate Raspberry Truffle Torte
with
Raspberry Coulis

◆

Coffee and Tea

A Celebration of New Beginnings

Three days ahead:
Prepare the **Rouille** for the **Salmon with Black Bean Salsa**. Put into "squeezer" container, cover and refrigerate.
Prepare flavored butters, if desired. Cover and refrigerate.
Prepare the **Raspberry Coulis** for the **Chocolate Raspberry Truffle Torte**. Cover and refrigerate.
Fold the napkins if desired.

Two days ahead:
Prepare the **Chocolate Raspberry Truffle Torte**. Cover and refrigerate.
Prepare the **Greek Lemon Soup**, cover and refrigerate.
Mince the parsley for the soup, rice and salsa. The parsley must be DRY. Cover and refrigerate.

The day before:
Purchase the fresh salmon and berries for dessert.
Wash the tomatoes for the **Black Bean Salsa**.
Prepare the **Black Bean Salsa** (without the tomatoes). Cover and refrigerate.
Put the flavored butter on its serving plate or bowl, cover and refrigerate.
Chill the wine and other cold beverages.
Set up coffee or tea tray, after dinner drinks, glasses, etc.
Make ice.
Set the table. Put out any non-food items (salt and pepper, wine coaster, etc.)
Arrange the flowers.

The morning before:
Prepare the dessert plates with cocoa powder garnish, if desired. Set aside.
Wash the berries and mint for the dessert garnish. Cover and refrigerate.
Unmold the **Chocolate Raspberry Truffle Torte** from the pan. Slice, dust with cocoa powder.
Set up coffee maker.

1-2 hours before guests arrive:
Chop the tomatoes; add to the **Black Bean Salsa**.
Prepare the **Make Ahead French-Style Rice**. Keep warm in 160°F oven.
Whip the cream for dessert. Decorate serving plates for **Chocolate Raspberry Truffle Torte**, set aside.
Remove butter from refrigerator to soften.
Slice purchased bread, if serving.
Ladle soup into serving bowls, refrigerate.

Before your guests arrive:
Remove **salmon** from refrigerator to allow to come to room temperature. Pat dry.
Preheat oven and baking sheet for salmon.
Preheat the plates and platters as needed.

After the guests arrive:
Garnish the soup; serve.
Sear and roast the salmon.
Stir the rice.
Plate the entrée.
Plate the dessert, garnish.

COOKING CLASS

"DOCTORED" STOCK

The best tasting stock is homemade, but quite often we just don't have time to make it. When you need good quality stock, but in a short period of time, you can make what I call "doctored" stock:

2 (15-ounce) cans good quality
 low-sodium broth or stock
4 or 5 chicken wings
 (if using chicken stock), or
 2 or 3 beef bones, from the
 butcher (if using beef stock)
1/2 medium onion
1 small carrot, in 1" chunks
1 stalk celery, in 1" chunks
1 clove garlic
4 black pepper corns
1 bay leaf
1 stalk parsley
1 branch fresh thyme or
 1/4 teaspoon dried thyme

Place all ingredients in a large saucepan; bring to a boil. Reduce heat to simmer, cook about 20 minutes. Pour hot stock through a strainer to remove vegetables and herbs. Makes about 3 cups stock.

The stock can be used immediately, refrigerated for two days, or frozen for up to two months. To destroy any pathogens ALWAYS reboil stock before use.

Greek Lemon Soup

A bowl full of golden, Greek Island summer sun, yet the heat of the summer is relieved by this light, cool, refreshing first course. On a cold fall or winter evening, you might want to serve this soup hot from the pot, as a reminder of the warmth of summer.

1 (14-½-ounce) can chicken stock
2 tablespoons long grain rice
zest and juice of one lemon
1 egg, at ROOM TEMPERATURE
1 tablespoon freshly minced parsley

In medium saucepan, heat stock to a boil. Stir in rice and lemon zest. Return the mixture to a boil. Lower the heat to simmer, cover and cook about 12 minutes, until the rice is tender.

Meanwhile, in a medium heatproof bowl, whisk together the lemon juice and egg. When the rice is done, ladle about ¼ cup of the hot stock onto the eggs, whisking to combine. Repeat twice more, and then pour the egg mixture into the pan with the remaining stock and rice. Chill thoroughly. *You can prepare the soup two days ahead store in an airtight container in refrigerator.* Serve sprinkled with freshly minced parsley.

Serves 4.

Pan-Seared Salmon
With Black Bean Salsa

The richness of salmon can stand up to the bold flavors of salsa and Rouille, showcasing a cornucopia of colors and flavors of the west and southwest. My favorite restaurant in Shirlington, Virginia, The Carlysle Grand Cafe, inspired this entree.

1 (1 – 1¼ pound) salmon fillet, skinned, or
    salmon steaks, skin and bones removed
1 tablespoon unsalted butter
1 tablespoon olive oil
salt and pepper
3 cups prepared Make Ahead French-style rice *(see recipe at sidebar)*
½ recipe Rouille *(recipe follows)*
1 recipe black bean salsa *(recipe follows)*
16 to 24 asparagus spears, steamed *(see sidebar on p. 43)*

Preheat oven and baking sheet to 425°F. Divide fillet into 4 serving portions if necessary; pat dry. Allow salmon to come to room temperature, about 15 minutes.

Heat butter and olive oil in large heavy skillet over high heat. Place fillets in heated pan, cook 2 minutes on each side, until golden brown. Remove to heated baking sheet; season with salt and pepper to taste. Place in preheated oven; cook 5 to 10 minutes, until internal temperature of salmon reaches 135°F. Remove from oven, tent with foil. Let stand 2 to 4 minutes, until internal temperature reaches 145°F. Serve immediately.

To serve: Pack rice into ramekin or small custard cup, unmold on center of HEATED dinner plate. Drizzle Rouille around edge of plate. Arrange asparagus spears in a spoke pattern around rice. Place salmon on rice, top with salsa. Serve immediately.

Serves 4.

To make this entree ahead, prepare rouille up to one week ahead. Cook asparagus according to directions on p. 43, up to two days ahead. Make black bean salsa one day in advance. Cook rice two hours ahead. Proceed with recipe as above.

TIMESAVERS!

MAKE AHEAD
FRENCH-STYLE RICE

*1 cup long grain rice
    (converted is OK, DO NOT
    use instant)
salt and freshly ground pepper
1 tablespoon butter
2 tablespoons freshly minced parsley*

In large pot, heat 1½ to 2 quarts of water to boiling. Add ½ teaspoon salt and the rice, stir. Boil 13 to 14 minutes, until rice is softened. Drain in sieve or colander. Place in heatproof serving dish, toss with butter and parsley, salt and pepper to taste. Tent with foil, to cover, but not tightly. You do not want the rice to steam. Place in preheated 160°F oven to hold, for up to two hours. Stir before serving.

Makes 3 cups cooked rice, serves 4.

Note: This method applies to Thai Jasmine and Basmati rice as well. If you prefer brown rice, using this method cook 20 to 24 minutes. Proceed as above.

PEPPER VINEGAR

Making your own pepper vinegar is so easy, and the result is beautiful.

1 cup cider vinegar
4 – 6 colorful fresh chilies
1 clove garlic

Place a clean, dry glass bottle or jar in a cold oven. Heat oven to 180°F. Meanwhile, in heatproof measure, heat vinegar in microwave on high 2 to 3 minutes, until VERY HOT. Wash and dry chilies. Peel garlic.

Carefully remove heated jar or bottle from oven. Slide chilies and garlic into hot jar. Pour hot vinegar over chilies to cover. Cap the bottle or jar tightly. Let stand until cool, top off with additional vinegar if necessary.

The vinegar will be flavored and ready for use in 5 to 7 days. Store tightly capped.

As you use the vinegar, replenish it with more vinegar to cover the chilies.

Black Bean Salsa

2 tomatoes, seeded and diced (*½ pound*)
¼ – ½ cup whole kernel corn (*see note below if using frozen corn*)
¼ cup black beans, rinsed and drained
2 tablespoons roasted red pepper, diced (*see sidebar on p. 54*)
2 green onions, thinly sliced
2 tablespoons canned chopped green chilies
1 clove garlic, minced
1 to 2 tablespoons pepper vinegar (*see sidebar at left*)
   or cider vinegar
½ tablespoon Extra-virgin olive oil
2 teaspoons minced parsley
½ teaspoon dried oregano
salt and pepper

Combine tomatoes, corn, beans, peppers, onions, chilies, garlic and vinegar. Add oil, parsley, and oregano. Salt and pepper to taste. Let stand 30 minutes, refrigerate to store.

Makes about 1½ cups salsa.

Note: If using frozen corn, rinse under cold water to thaw, drain well.

Note: To make salsa one day in advance, combine all ingredients EXCEPT TOMATOES. Add the tomatoes no more than 4 hours before serving or they tend to get mushy.

Low-Fat Rouille or Red Pepper Mayonnaise

This beautiful pink sauce complements the flavors of fish, as well as sandwiches, asparagus and artichokes. It is a staple in my refrigerator. It is pronounced roo-EE.

1½ cups low-fat or non-fat Mayonnaise
2 cloves garlic, minced
6 – 8 tablespoons minced or pureed roasted red pepper
   (see sidebar on p. 54)
1 – 3 tablespoons pepper vinegar *(see sidebar on p. 140)*
or white wine vinegar, or cider vinegar
⅛ – ¼ teaspoon cayenne pepper or hot pepper sauce, to taste
salt

Combine Mayonnaise, garlic, and pepper puree. Slowly add vinegar, until desired consistency and tartness is reached. Correct seasonings with cayenne pepper or hot pepper sauce and salt. Refrigerate. *The Rouille will keep 3 to 4 weeks.*

Makes about 2 cups Rouille.

EXTRA TOUCHES

FLAVORED MAYONNAISE

Rouille is just one example of a flavored Mayonnaise. Try experimenting with a few other combinations. To 1 cup of the best quality prepared Mayonnaise, add:

For Aioli;
(Pronounced I-OH-lee, French for Garlic Mayonnaise)

1 – 2 cloves finely minced garlic
a few drops hot pepper sauce

For Lime Aioli:

1 – 2 cloves finely minced garlic
½ teaspoon finely grated lime zest
1 teaspoon freshly squeezed
   lime juice

For Rosemary Aioli:

1 – 2 cloves finely minced garlic
½ teaspoon finely minced
   fresh rosemary

For Tartar Sauce:

1 teaspoon capers
1 teaspoon finely minced dill pickle
1 teaspoon finely minced onion

Chocolate Raspberry Truffle Torte

Rich chocolate…sinful. Tart raspberries…sensual. Luscious and beautiful. This torte is a variation on a recipe, which I have made for many years and always gotten rave reviews. It is unbelievably easy to prepare.

1 cup butter, plus a bit for the pan
1½ cups sugar
16 ounces semi-sweet chocolate, chopped
¾ cup plus 2 tablespoons unsweetened raspberry puree
    with NO SEEDS *(see Fruit Purees on p. 152)*
6 eggs, at room temperature
6 egg yolks, at room temperature
¼ cup raspberry liqueur *(such as Framboise, see sidebar on p. 28)*
1 teaspoon raspberry extract (optional)
boiling water for water bath
unsweetened cocoa powder, for garnish
slightly sweetened raspberry coulis
whipped cream (optional)
fresh raspberries, for garnish
mint leaves

Preheat oven to 325°F. Generously butter the bottom and sides of a 9 to 10-inch springform pan. Line bottom of pan with parchment paper *(see sidebar on p. 89)*, butter paper. Wrap outside of pan in heavy-duty foil, taking care not to make holes, set aside.

Melt 1 cup butter and sugar in heavy saucepan over low heat until sugar dissolves. Add chopped chocolate pieces; stir until smooth. Remove from heat; stir in raspberry puree. Cool to just warm to touch.

Whisk eggs and yolks in a large bowl just until combined. Gradually whisk in chocolate/raspberry mixture. Add liqueur. Pour batter into prepared springform pan, place pan in larger baking pan. Place in oven; pour boiling water into the outer pan to a depth of one inch. Bake in preheated oven until edges of torte puff slightly but center is not completely set, about 1 hour. DO NOT OVERBAKE (torte will continue to set as it cools). Carefully remove from water bath; remove outer foil. Cool on a rack. Cover and refrigerate overnight or up to one week.

Run a small knife around the side of the pan to loosen. Carefully release pan sides. Sift cocoa powder over torte, if desired. Cut into wedges, wiping knife clean before each cut. You may make cutting the torte easier by heating the knife under very hot water, then drying before each cut. Garnish the wedges with raspberry coulis, whipped cream rosettes, fresh raspberries and mint.

Serves 16.

TIMESAVERS!

This recipe can be divided in half, and baked in two 6 or 7 inch springform pans if you like. Serve one, freeze the other for another dinner.

This is a great torte to cut into serving sized wedges, wrap individually and freeze for future use. Thaw overnight in the refrigerator before serving.

Show-Offs!!

When you are feeling more confident
in your entertaining skills, or if you just
want to add something else, a little extra
touch is appreciated. And if you want to
knock their socks off, these are the most
exciting, bang-for-your-buck, little things
you can do to really polish it up!

Show-Offs!!

GARNISHING AND PRESENTATION

FLAVORED OR COMPOUND BUTTERS

DESSERT SAUCES

FRUIT PUREES

SIMPLE GARNISHES

DESSERT GARNISHES

CENTERPIECES, DECORATIONS AND SETTING THE STAGE

NAPKIN FOLDS

BUFFETS

PAIRING FOOD AND WINE

Garnishing and Presentation

We've all heard the phrase "Presentation is 90%." Well, that may not be exactly true. While we do 'eat with our eyes first', a beautiful plate will never substitute for good food. The best presentation of any dish should always start with properly prepared food. Basic cooking techniques make most foods visually appealing. Much like a painting, the garnish and presentation is the frame for the piece.

It is easiest to arrange food so that it garnishes itself. This is known as presentation or the way the food is "presented" on the plate. As you lay it out, heed the principles of variety and contrast. Good food presentation actually begins with a plan that incorporates foods that, while being compatible, differ from one another in color, size, shape and texture. Do not crowd the food, let each item contrast with its background and stand apart on its own stage. Keep this in mind when planning your appetizer, entree and dessert menus. It will help you to avoid at serving time a plate consisting of a "chunk" of meat, a "chunk" of potato and a "chunk" of vegetable. This isn't a very pleasing presentation, it lacks interest. Likewise, a little planning and you can have a glorious dessert plate for your guests.

When planning the appetizer, entree or dessert menus, I like to follow two basic rules: keep it simple, and do as much ahead as possible. Many sauces can be prepared in advance, especially those used for desserts. Possibly the appetizer or dessert can be portioned out ahead of time. Some garnishes can also be done beforehand; just make sure they don't look "tired" before putting them on the plate.

Once the items on the dinner plate have been thoughtfully selected, properly cooked and tastefully arranged, it may be time for sauce. You may choose to present the sauce over the food, or *over saucing*. Over saucing can lead to *too much saucing*. Sauces and gravies are meant to enhance the flavor of food, not obscure it. Thick sauces should be ladled over the food in a ribbon. Thin sauces can be slightly more generously applied. If needed, extra sauce can be presented at the table in a sauceboat.

Another approach to saucing is called *under saucing*. First, lay the sauce down on the plate, and then place the food into the sauce, letting the sauce frame the food from below. This popular and attractive technique can be very striking when two sauces are used. Under saucing is most successful with sauces that compliment each other, and are of similar consistency though different colors. For techniques to present two sauces see the sidebar on "Dessert Garnishes" in this section. Quite often, you can do the saucing technique beforehand, and set the plates aside.

If you choose to add a garnish to your plate, it should be **appealing to the eye**, as well as **echo or compliment the flavor** of the dish. And only one garnish per plate, please. More than one is fussy. The general rule is that the garnish is served at the same temperature as the food. Garnishing is usually done at the last minute. If you garnish a dish and then let it set in the refrigerator for several hours, the garnish won't look as fresh as it should. But many garnishes can be made ahead and stored in airtight containers for a few hours, ready to go on the plates. For more ideas on garnishes, check the "Simple Garnishes" page in this section. If you want to get even more elaborate, I suggest you purchase a book on garnishing.

In keeping it simple, it is easy to remember that the presentation is more important than the garnish. How will the plate look? The plate is your canvas for showcasing the food. A flat plate is not appealing. Stacking foods can create a bit of **vertical height**. Remember the stylish restaurant presentations? Just don't overdo it. Straight lines are not as attractive as **angles**. **Curves** are appealing. Straight lines can easily be achieved with a knife; curves are already present in most foods. Visualize the beautiful curve in an apple slice or the graceful oval of a grape half. These are nature's gifts. Use them to your advantage.

The same applies to the buffet table: **elevate** some of your dishes, food sculptures, the centerpiece, with simple pedestals covered with extra linen. Footed cake servers and tiered trays also add height to your table. Place serving dishes on the buffet back from the edge of the table by six inches or so. This will prevent most spills from dropping onto the floor, and from soiling your guest's clothes. But don't line the dishes up in a single line. Remember that you want to create angles and curves. If your table looks too sparse, fill in some of the empty space with stems of ivy, ferns, kale, chicory, evergreen, vegetable flowers, or other items related to your menu or the season.

Let's talk about serving dishes. A few common sense guidelines will help in arranging food in these vessels so they are attractive and easily served. Plates, platters and bowl should look full and bountiful. DO NOT OVERFILL. Simple and elegant is a good rule of thumb.

Fill deep dished bowls above the level of the rim, in a mounded shape to create height. If you use food as a border or as part of a design laid onto the surface of the food, it should be one of the ingredients of the dish itself or at least be very complimentary to it. Foods look larger and more striking when framed in a complete border. However, a partial border going around the back of the dish, serving as a crown will work almost as well.

Garnishing and presentation can be fun and easy. Close attention, sharp knives, quality ingredients and a little practice will assure your success. So relax and…play with your food!

BUTTER ROLLS

When your flavored butter is finished, you will want the best way to store it. First, tear off a square of waxed paper, about 12" X 12". Scoop the butter mixture onto the paper, in a vertical line down the center of the paper. Now, fold the right side of the paper over the left, lining up the leading edges, so that the butter is running down the folding area.

Using a very large knife with your right hand, press the top layer of paper into the butter with the dull side of the blade next to the butter. Tightly hold the edge of the paper on the bottom. Pull the knife to the left, tightening the roll to the desired size.

Finish by rolling the paper around the roll, twisting the ends. Refrigerate to set up. Then, unroll and slice thinly to serve in small rounds, or scoop with a small melon baller to form balls.

Flavored or Compound Butters

Just an extra little touch to make a meal more elegant, whether paired with appropriate food or simply served with bread. These butters are a beautiful addition to your table setting.

These butters are easily made with a fork by hand or in a food processor, and can be made well in advance. I recommend using unsalted butter for these recipes. Let the butter come to room temperature for fast, easy mixing. Begin by stirring the butter, then add all the flavoring ingredients, and mix well.

Shape in a long roll in waxed paper *(see sidebar at left)*. Store in refrigerator up to two weeks, or freeze for up to six months.

Lemon Pepper Butter (Serve with vegetables, grilled meats, chicken or fish, bread, etc.):

½ cup butter
½ teaspoon salt
a few grinds freshly cracked pepper
½ to 1 teaspoon freshly squeezed lemon juice

Herb Butter (Serve with vegetables, potatoes, rice, grilled meat, fish or poached chicken.):

½ cup butter
½ teaspoon salt
1 tablespoon each: shallot, parsley, tarragon, chives, and chervil; or
    your own combination of herbs

Sun-Dried Tomato Butter (Serve on grilled meat, chicken, or spread on bread and grill.):

½ cup butter
½ teaspoon salt
dash hot pepper sauce
2 – 3 tablespoons sun-dried tomatoes, chopped
1 teaspoon tomato paste

Snail Butter (*Not because it has snails in it, but because it is commonly served with Escargot. Serve on green beans, rice, potatoes, shellfish, grilled or sautéed meats or fish.*):

½ cup butter
½ teaspoon salt
½ teaspoon minced shallot
½ teaspoon minced garlic
2 tablespoons minced parsley
dash nutmeg
pepper, to taste

Mustard Butter (Serve on boiled meats and chicken.):

½ cup butter
½ teaspoon salt
2 teaspoons Dijon mustard

Red Pepper Butter (Serve on vegetables, fish, bread):

½ cup butter
½ teaspoon salt
2-3 tablespoons red pepper puree or coulis *(see recipe on p. 54)*

Raspberry Butter (Serve on breakfast breads, scones.):

½ cup butter
pinch of salt
4 tablespoons raspberry puree *(see sidebar on p. 152)*
2 – 3 tablespoons confectioner's sugar (to taste)

Maple Butter (Serve on pancakes, waffles, etc.):

½ cup butter
pinch of salt
4 tablespoons real maple syrup

TECHNIQUE

PEELING GARLIC

Peeling garlic can be a chore, but it doesn't have to be. Just strike each clove with the heal of your hand or the side of your chef's knife. The papery skin will loosen, and pull away easily.

KNOW YOUR INGREDIENTS

CHOCOLATE

*With a little knowledge and understanding, you can select the right **chocolate** and store it properly.*

Good quality eating chocolate is made up of cocoa solids, cocoa butter, sugar, and vanillin to enhance the flavor. An emulsifier may be added, as well as milk solids. The better the quality of chocolate, the higher the percentage of cocoa solids and cocoa butter to the other ingredients. Lesser quality chocolate will substitute vegetable oils for the cocoa butter, and typically use less cocoa solids, more sugar. The vegetable oils will leave a greasy taste and feel in your mouth. Buy the best quality chocolate available. Read the label and check the ingredients so that you won't be fooled.

Bitter or unsweetened chocolate is simply ground cocoa solids and cocoa butter with possibly an emulsifier. It provides intense chocolate flavor in recipes.

Bittersweet and semi-sweet chocolate have more cocoa butter and sugar added. Semi-sweet chocolate has slightly more sugar added than bittersweet. These two can be interchanged in recipes.

Milk chocolate has cocoa butter, sugar and milk solids added and may contain lecithin for smoothness.

White chocolate contains no cocoa solids; it is a mixture of cocoa butter, sugar, milk solids and lecithin.

Store chocolate in a cool dry place, at 55 to 68°F, tightly wrapped. Milk and white chocolate products generally stay fresh well over a year when stored properly. Dark chocolate will keep 2-3 years!

Truly Decadent Chocolate Sauce

The name says it all.

½ cup heavy cream*
4 ounces semi-sweet chocolate, finely chopped

Bring cream to boil, remove from heat. Stir in chopped chocolate; let stand 2 minutes. Whisk until sauce becomes smooth and shiny, about 2 to 3 minutes. Serve warm or at room temperature.

Makes 1 cup sauce.

Note: This sauce can be made ahead 1 to 2 weeks and refrigerated, but it will set up. Before using, you will need to reheat the sauce and stir. The sauce may also be frozen for up to 6 months. You may need only ½ recipe, depending on your choice of presentation.

*Substituting whole milk for the cream can make a slightly lower-fat version of this sauce. However, DO NOT BOIL the milk. Add the chocolate to the milk and heat slowly, stirring until the sauce is smooth and shiny. Serve warm or at room temperature. Refrigerate covered.

Crème Anglaise

This is a rich custard sauce, which lends itself to a multitude of flavorings. It is a wonderfully versatile dessert sauce.

1 cup milk
vanilla pod, split, seeds scraped out (*optional depending on flavor choice, see below*)
3 egg yolks
⅓ cup sugar

Prepare an ice bath: in a large bowl, place ice cubes and cold water. Set near the stove.

In a heavy-bottomed pan over medium heat, slowly bring milk, vanilla pod and seeds to a boil. Meanwhile, in large bowl, whisk yolks and sugar until well combined and pale in color. Slowly pour hot milk mixture into egg mixture, whisking constantly. Check the bottom of the pan. If ANY of the milk mixture has scorched, wash the pan.

Return the mixture to the pan over low heat, stir with a wooden spoon until it is thickened and coats back of the spoon. Immediately place bottom of pan in the ice bath to cool quickly. Stir in flavoring variation, if desired. Pass through a sieve. Store covered in refrigerator, up to 2 days.

*VARIATIONS:

Coffee: *Add 1-⅓ teaspoons instant coffee to milk and add 1 teaspoon Kahlua or Creme de Cacao at the end.*

Chocolate: *Add in 3 or 4 ounces of finely chopped semi-sweet chocolate at the end, stir to melt.*

For the following variations, leave out the vanilla pod and seeds at the beginning of the recipe:

Liqueurs: *Add 2 tablespoons of liqueur at the end.*

Citrus Fruits: *Make an infusion by heating 1 tablespoon grated zest (see sidebar on p. 27) with the milk, or use 1 teaspoon extract, added at the end.*

Butterscotch: *Replace granulated sugar with brown sugar.*

Pistachio: *Toast ¾ ounce chopped pistachio nuts under a broiler for 3 to 4 minutes, shaking VERY OFTEN to prevent burning. Cool. Grind nuts to a fine paste or powder. Whisk the pistachio paste into the prepared cream while still warm.*

KNOW YOUR INGREDIENTS

VANILLA PODS

Vanilla pods or beans *are the long, thin dark brown fruit of the vanilla orchid, most of which come from Madagascar. The dried pods can be found in the spice section of larger supermarkets or specialty shops. They should be stored in an airtight container.*

To use the pod, slice it in half lengthwise and use the tip of the knife to scrape out the seeds. These seeds are the characteristic brown specks that you see in French vanilla ice cream. You may choose to use only the seeds to flavor your dish, saving the pod for another use. Or you may use both for added flavor.

Put the saved pod in a small jar and cover it with sugar. Seal the jar and let the sugar stand for about a week — now you have vanilla sugar. This is great for sprinkling on desserts or fresh fruit.

Fruit Purees or Coulis

A coulis is a thick puree made from fruit or vegetable, or the thick juices from cooked meats. Fruit coulis are usually sweetened; vegetable coulis are typically seasoned with herbs and or spices.

Fruit purees or coulis are easily prepared and are a very versatile addition to any dessert tray. Their flavors are clear and bold, providing visual and flavorful accents to your food. A less sweet fruit puree can provide a refreshing balance to a sweet cake.

When drizzled over foods the term for presentation is "over sauce." The plate can also be visually stunning if the puree is under the food like a puddle, performing as an "under sauce." This effect is especially dramatic when paired with a second fruit puree, a creme Anglaise or other flavored sauce. And fruit purees make excellent flavorings for mousses and whipped creams.

Fruit purees can be produced from fresh, frozen or occasionally canned fruit. Typically, a fruit puree is not sweetened, but a coulis has sugar added.

First, select good quality fruit. For each cup of fruit you will need between 2 tablespoons and ½ cup of sugar to make coulis, depending on the sweetness of the fruit and your own tastes. Bear in mind that the coulis will taste sweeter when heated than when tasted cold.

For berries or currants, wash, dry, and heat just to a boil, with a bit of sugar if desired. The process of heating to a boil destroys any enzymes or pathogens that will quickly spoil your puree. Pass the mixture through a sieve to remove the seeds. Check for sweetness and add more sugar if necessary. Finish with a teaspoon or two of freshly squeezed lemon juice to bring out the fresh flavor of the fruit if you like. Fruit purees and coulis can be refrigerated for a week, or frozen up to 6 months. If you like to use small portions, try freezing in an ice cube tray, then storing in a zip-top plastic bag.

Mango, guava, papaya, or passion fruit also make beautiful purees and coulis. Just peel, seed and chop the fruit then cook as outlined above, with sugar if desired. Blend the mixture in a blender or food processor until smooth. Kiwi makes an especially lovely and versatile puree. Peel and process just until smooth, trying not to break up the black seeds. I like to leave them in, for color. Then cook the kiwi with sugar, just like berries.

Fresh fruits that brown easily like bananas, peaches or pears, or those having a high water content such as melons are obviously not a good choice for purees. To obtain a lovely puree of peaches or pears, start with canned fruit, drain the syrup and process as above. Add reserved syrup if necessary to thin.

THE RIGHT TOOLS

*A good way to store and pour purees is by using a "**squeezer**" container available at restaurant suppliers, or a hair-coloring bottle from the beauty supply store.*

Simple Garnishes

green onions – thin diagonal slices, use a strip of green as a tie
  for vegetable bundles *(see recipe on p. 108)*
tomatoes – half-cups, fans
cucumbers – fans
carrot – triangles, curls
pepper – strips, fans, triangles
onion – flowers
avocado – fans, or finely diced
eggplant – fans
radicchio – cups, just choose the small leaves

strawberry – halves, quarters, fans
grapes – halves, sugared
lemon – wedges, twists
pear – fans or thin slices

bread – croutons, toast points, crumbs
rice – pack in ramekin, turn out gently to hold shape
tortillas – cups, thin fried strips, wedges
butter – shapes, balls, piped rosettes

For platter bases, first spread with your choice of: salal leaves, citrus leaves, shredded raddichio, cabbage, spinach leaves or other greens. Then top with your recipe.

To decorate the rim of a plate or platter, lightly sprinkle with your choice of: paprika, minced parsley, curry or chili powder. This can be done in advance, if you have an area to leave the plates laid out.

(see recipe on p. 108)

COOKING CLASS

Carrot or pepper triangles:
Cut a rectangular piece of vegetable from a thin slice. Then, make two parallel cuts.

Now, fold into a triangle shape.

For onion flowers:
Cut an onion in half crosswise. Then, make a series of cuts almost all the way through; creating "flower petals." Let onion stand in ice water to allow petal to open.

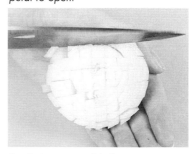

For fruit or vegetable fans:
Cut thin slices, leaving a small bit attached at the stem end. Press and fan out.

Dust the plates:

Citrus swans:

Dessert Garnishes

dust center or rim of plate or top of dessert with:
    confectioner's sugar
    cocoa powder
    cinnamon
    nutmeg

fruit garnishes:
    strawberry halves, quarters, fans, or whole *(see sidebar on p. 44)*
    raspberries or blackberries, dusted with confectioner's sugar
    grapes or currants, crusted with granulated sugar
    blueberries
    slice of star fruit (carambola)
    very finely sliced apple wedges
    citrus wedges, twists, swans, zest

don't forget:
    nuts, chopped, whole, slivers, etc.
    fresh mint sprigs
    edible flowers
    chocolate sticks (purchased)
    chocolate covered coffee beans (purchased)
    whipped cream rosettes
    pastry shapes, cut with cookie cutters

fruit purees, sauces**:
  drizzle over
  puddle
  pair, puddle one, design with another:
    feather, spider web, hearts
"paint" shapes or "modern art" on plate:
    circles, hearts, teardrops, squiggles

***When designing with two different purees or sauces, they must be of similar consistency or one will float on the other instead of making a lovely design.*

easy sauces (purchase already prepared):
  chocolate syrup
  caramel sauce
  maple syrup
creme fraiche or sour cream, sweetened and thinned with
    a little milk

Make a puddle of one sauce, then design with a second.
Feathering: draw parallel lines with the second sauce, then draw a knifepoint through.

Spider web design: draw a spiral from the center, then feather with a knifepoint.

Hearts: drop circles of second sauce, then draw knifepoint through to create hearts.

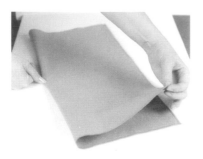

Step 1

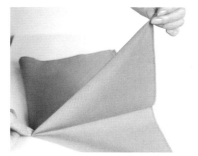

Step 2

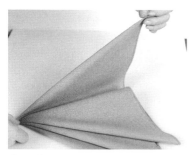

Step 3

Step 4

Rippling Fan Napkin Fold

This napkin fold is particularly effective when the napkin contrasts with the table linen or the plate on which it is displayed. Add drama to your place setting by using this napkin under a plate.

Step 1: Fold the napkin in half to form a rectangle. Place the fold so that it is along the bottom edge. Place you thumb at the center point of the fold at the bottom. Grasp the top layer at the upper right corner.

Step 2: Pull up the top right corner until the bottom forms into a triangle, as pictured. Place top triangle back down, slightly to the left to begin forming the fan.

Step 3: Now grasp the top layer of the upper left corner, pulling up to form a triangle. Then place it to the right, atop the two already formed, continuing to form the fan.

Step 4: Grasp the top corner of the remaining triangle on the left, and fold it to the right, to finish the fan.

Step 5: Adjust the folds evenly, then press the fan if desired.

Step 5

Centerpieces and Setting the Stage

Decorating for your dinner party should be part of the fun! This is the "presentation and garnish" for the table! And the best part is that it can be done in advance, so that you are not rushed. With a little creativity and some practice you will find it easy to utilize what you already have in your home. Yes, it is easy and acceptable to just purchase a floral bouquet and be done with it, but you can do so much more! Soon, you will find that you have much more in your bag of tricks than just flowers.

When you are decorating your table for your dinner party, think in odd numbers as they are much more interesting — five candles or lanterns, three figurines. Use what you have on hand, pulling items from your home-decorating scheme. Maybe the figurines you have on the coffee table could become part of your centerpiece. If the dinner is centered on a theme, use something relating to it. Bedding plants crowded into a basket are appropriate to the current season. You could use strands of fresh ivy from your garden for napkin rings. A pottery pitcher filled with long spaghetti, some beautiful peppers scattered about, and different types of small pasta scattered like confetti on the table for an Italian dinner. Scatter beautiful fall leaves and nuts for an autumn dinner. How about a silver bowl filled to overflowing with bright green apples or lush lemons. I have scattered sand in the center of my dining room table, placed pillar candles in the sand and seashells for a summer evening. Do you have a collection of something? Do you see where I'm going with this? Let your imagination be your guide. Don't forget that you should be able to see your guests over the center-piece, so keep the height to a reasonable level. And candles are always a nice touch in the evening. They should be lit for the meal.

Linens can be very formal, the lace tablecloth and all. Or you might find some unconventional items useful in setting your table. How about using bandanas for placemats and napkins for a country theme possibly for a gourmet picnic? They come in assorted bright colors and are relatively inexpensive. If you don't have enough placemats and napkins of one color, try mixing and matching two sets. This is a consideration when purchasing linens in the future. Keep in mind what you already have, then purchase things with the idea in mind to mix with it.

Mixing and matching can work well not only with linens, but with dishes, candlesticks, or serving pieces. With a little thought and planning, soon you will have an inventory of great party items that will work for many occasions.

Buffets

Buffet style service is by far the easiest for you. MAKE IT SIMPLE for your guests as well, by making it easy for them. I suggest that appetizers be presented in a separate area, possibly the living room. Then the main course. The dessert should be served separately, not presented at the same time as the entree.

Your buffet should be arranged in a logical order — it's just common sense. Have you ever tried to balance a tray with flatware and a beverage, while filling a plate? Take a walk through your buffet set-up, and make any necessary adjustments. Arrange the buffet so the dinner plates are first, food second, trays (if you are using them) and silver last. Check the traffic flow: will those waiting to help themselves be crowding the exit door?

Be sure that each guest has a place to sit. You may want to consider allowing your guests to serve themselves the main course at a buffet, then seating everyone at the dining room table if space allows. You can set the table ahead just as for a sit-down dinner, except for the plates. This way your guests will have less to juggle to the table.

As host or hostess, you should serve the beverages. This will save on your carpet cleaning bill and the embarrassment of your guests as well. You can serve each guest after he or she is seated, minimizing the risk of a toppled drink. Now, down to the nitty-gritty of set-up.

Table Coverings

If your buffet table has beautiful wood grain, you may want to leave it uncovered, but beware of potential damage from food and wine spills. Be sure to have thick, protective mats under the serving pieces to protect the surface and to keep the dishes from slipping. If the table is covered, the cloth should be large enough to hang well over the sides and ends. If your table linens are too small, consider a king-size sheet, crisply pressed.

Centerpieces

Fresh flowers or fruit provide great color or you may choose to use something more creative *(see the section on centerpieces in the Show-Offs!! section for more ideas)*. No matter what you choose, be sure to make the arrangement large. A skimpy centerpiece on a large table looks silly. A centerpiece for a seated dinner table should be low enough for guests to easily see over. But a buffet table is viewed from a standing position and needs more height to be interesting and inviting. Put that centerpiece on a pedestal or make it taller, but don't sacrifice stability. You don't want it to fall over if someone bumps the table! Raising the centerpiece up will also allow more room on the table for food.

The Circular Buffet

If your buffet table occupies the center of the room allowing guest access to all sides, you will use a circular buffet plan. Most people, being right-handed, find a clockwise flow of traffic easier to serve themselves. At the starting point guests should find dinner plates, stacked near the main course. The serving spoon or fork is placed near the main dish. Next in line, on the left, would be the vegetables, then salad, and relishes. The appropriate serving spoon should be placed near each dish. Following around the table, your guests should come to salt and pepper, bread and butter. And lastly, napkins and flatware. In setting the buffet table, allow ample room in front of or between dishes for your guests to rest their plates. It is extremely awkward to try to serve yourself salad with only one hand.

The Three-sided Buffet

If your room has limited floor space, you may opt to place the buffet table against the wall. This will cut down on the usable food serving space, but allow more room for a spectacular centerpiece or backdrop. The table arrangement is pretty much the same as for a circular buffet, beginning with the dinner plates, main course, vegetable, etc. It is easier for your guests to serve themselves moving from right to left, just as in the circular buffet. Of course, these basic plans can be modified to suit your needs, but remember two important principles: food should be placed in easy reach and arranged in a logical pattern so that your guests are not bumping into one another.

Think about how your guests will serve themselves and present the food accordingly. If an item requires cutting to provide individual portions, then cut it before placing it on the buffet table. And just a tip: if you use a footed plate or bowl to present a dish, be sure that it is not likely to topple as your guests take their portions.

Short on Space?

If you are short on space, the food for a buffet does not have to be presented all in one place. The hot food may be located near the stove or oven; the cold items could be in the dining area. The napkins and flatware could be placed in the area where your guests will be sitting, just so they are handy.

Coffee Service

If you choose to have a buffet area for coffee as well, I would suggest setting it up on another surface or table, again bearing in mind the potential damage to wood and carpet. You may want to consider setting out cups, saucers and spoons, then circulating with a tray with the coffeepot, cream and sugar. An added advantage to serving guests yourself is that you will always know that the coffee is hot, and when you are running low.

The Circular Buffet

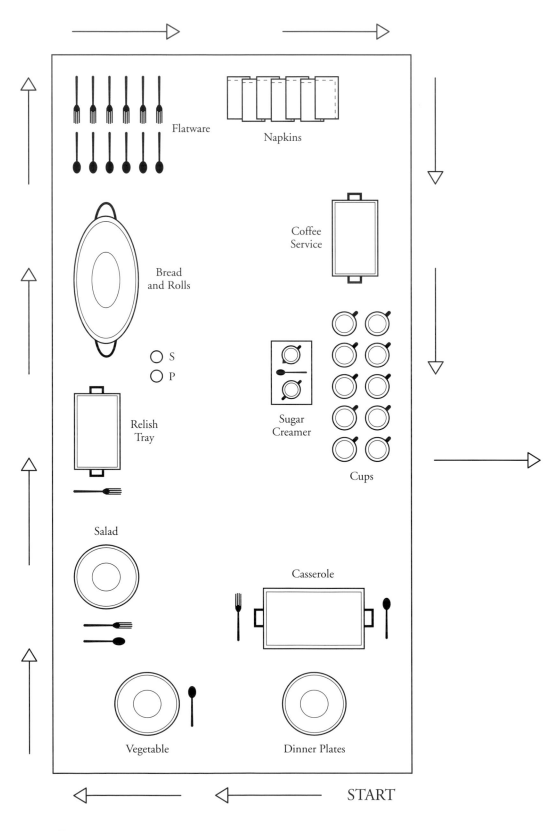

Flatware

Napkins

Coffee
Service

Bread
and Rolls

S
P

Relish
Tray

Sugar
Creamer

Cups

Salad

Casserole

Vegetable

Dinner Plates

START

The Three-Sided Buffet

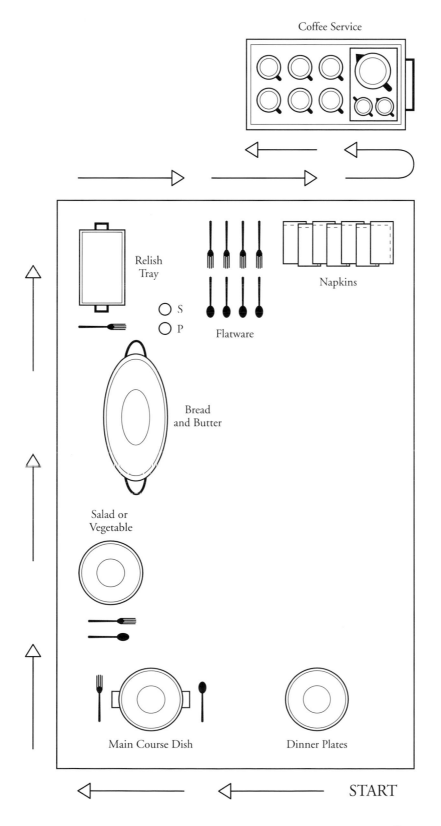

Coffee Service

Relish Tray

S
P

Flatware

Napkins

Bread and Butter

Salad or Vegetable

Main Course Dish

Dinner Plates

START

Pairing Food and Wine

Okay. The difficult question. What wine should you serve? What wine will best compliment the menu you have chosen? Today's food and wine paring rules suggest the best wine to pair with your food is the wine you enjoy most. If the flavors of the food are balanced and the flavor of the wine is good, this will work well. If you are a wine novice experimentation can be fun, but sometimes you want a sure thing. When you need help there are two basic rules of thumb:

Serve red wine with meat, white wine with fish.

Hearty, heavier foods need hearty, heavier wines; light, delicate foods need lighter, more delicate wines.

When in doubt, follow the rules. Or when you are a bit more confident, break them. They are simply guidelines, and you should drink what you like. But sometimes things can get a bit confusing. What wine do you serve with a hearty chicken dish, braised in tomato sauce? Or with spicy foods, like Thai? A suggestion: ask the wine expert at the store. Making a connection with a good wine merchant can be invaluable, whether he or she is at a wine specialty shop or at your local supermarket.

I cannot stress enough "Do not be intimidated." Just because someone tells you a wine is good or bad doesn't always make it so. Just as not everyone likes squash, or chocolate, or strawberries, not everyone will feel the same way about a particular wine. If you like a certain wine, then it is a good wine. And if it doesn't taste good to you then it's not a good wine. We all taste things differently including wine. Don't worry if you cannot taste a particular element someone may have used to describe a wine: smokiness, cherries, citrus. You are most likely tasting things that they cannot, even if you can't describe these flavors.

Price is not necessarily an indication of quality. If you like a wine, then it is a good wine, regardless of price. Is a $100 bottle of wine ten times as good as a $10 bottle — probably not. It may be better, even a lot better, but there is no guarantee.

And one more thing: if you are choosing a wine to use in a sauce or marinade, keep in mind that if it doesn't taste good in a glass, it won't taste good as a marinade or sauce. It is simpler and customary to use the same variety of wine for sauce or marinade as for serving with the food. Cooking wine should be decent quality, but it need not be the same exact wine should you choose to serve a better wine with dinner. The subtle nuances of a great wine will be lost in the cooking — don't waste it.

How do you know what's in that bottle? In the United States as well as Australia, New Zealand, South Africa and Chile, wines are *varietals* — which means they are named according to the variety of grapes from which the wine has been made. European wines are named for the *appellation* or region in which the grapes were grown. Because Americans are more familiar with *varietal* wines, I will deal with them in this manner.

White wines can be made with either white or red grapes, but are rarely fermented and aged as long as the reds. Whites tend to be younger, and are meant to be drunk earlier than reds. White wines don't need the aging necessary for reds to smooth out the rough edges, to soften the tannins, which are those substances in red wine that can make it bitter. Tannins come from fermenting the red wine with the skins of the red grapes and from the oak barrels in which it is aged.

White wines tend to have more acid, and taste better colder. Think fruit juice; it tastes much better cold than at room temperature. However, cold temperatures amplify the tannins, so red wines benefit by being served a bit warmer, near room temperature. A dramatic example is tea, which has a lot of tannins. It is much smoother served hot, but tends to have more of a bite when served ice cold. Generally speaking, the lighter the white wine, the colder it should be served.

So, what to choose. When talking about matching food with wine, the idea is to keep the wine similar to the food. The food should not overpower the wine; the wine should not overpower the food. Spicy food goes with spicy wine. Rich, complex food needs similar wine. Foods cooked with a lot of herbs tend to pair better with those wines with herbal characteristics. A good source of information about the wine you are considering is the label, many of which describe the wine's intrinsic flavors: are they sweet, acidic, bitter (high in tannins), oaky, buttery (rich, higher alcohol content)? Sweeter wines complement spicy, savory or salty foods, but when paired with overly sweet foods will taste sour by comparison. Wines with higher acidity, or tartness, are great amplifiers of the subtle flavors in foods. They are a nice match for acidic foods, those with lemon juice or vinegar. Wines high in tannin match well with foods that have a bit of bitter edge to their own flavors, like blackened foods, or foods from the grill. The bitterness of a high tannin wine can be a good counter balance to rich, fatty foods like cheese. Most full-bodied Chardonnays and red wines like Chianti, Sangiovese, Rioja and Cabernet Sauvignon are aged in oak barrels, which gives these wines their characteristic oak flavor. Rich meats or oily fish like salmon, with rich sauces are best complemented by these wines. The richness of these wines is attributed to their higher alcohol content, which will amplify salt and spice.

The varietals

Let's begin with the whites, which tend to be lighter than reds. The lightest are the Champagne and sparkling wines. The drier or less sweet versions of these wines stand well on their own, or paired with light appetizers such as smoked salmon or oysters. The slightly sweeter version compliments lighter, sweeter foods, a great pair for fruit desserts. Sparkling Rosés fall into this grouping. Champagne and sparkling wines should always be served very well chilled.

Hot and spicy Mexican, Thai, Indian and tangy foods are well matched by Sauvignon Blanc, with its refreshingly crisp citrus and herbal flavors. Sauvignon Blanc is another of those wines, which can be light or medium bodied, depending on the producer. Sauvignon Blanc is well suited to those dishes containing garlic, herbs or ginger, goat cheese or tomatoes. Think pesto.

Semillon, a more round yet sharp, zesty wine feels heavier in your mouth. Most often you will find it blended with another varietal, maybe a Sauvignon Blanc to add more flavor and body to the wine. Semillon and its blends are nice compliments to shellfish, mussels, oysters and fowl.

Pinot Gris or Pinot Grigio is similar to Sauvignon Blanc, fruitier but without the herbs. It is an excellent all-purpose wine for appetizers and lunches. Pinot Gris/Grigio balances well with richer foods because of its higher acidity. The characteristics of fruit and acid match this wine with seafood in strong sauces, fattier seafood such as salmon or smoked salmon, and veal,

With slightly more body, Gewürztraminer, pronounced *ga-VIRTS-tra-meener,* is an easily recognized wine because of its distinctive flavor. *Gewurz* in German means *spice,* which is the main characteristic of the wine. It is typically quite dry, with a hint of sweetness, topped with the unmistakable spice, but not overpowering. Its aroma is sweet, but the flavor is not. Gewürztraminer can be paired very successfully with spicy fare: sausages or salami, Thai, Szechwan, other Chinese foods or barbecue.

I will veer away from the varietals for a brief moment to mention Trebbiano, a dry, medium-bodied white from Italy. This wine has a fruity aroma yet is dry, not quite as spicy as a German Gewürztraminer. It is a lovely compliment to chicken picatta or Asian foods.

The German style white wines, known as Rieslings, pronounced *REEZ-ling,* can be dry or slightly sweet, but their primary characteristic is fruity and flowery, sweetness and light. Some Rieslings can be very light, others more flavorful. Riesling matches well with crab, scallops, prawns, turkey or pork loin. The slight sweetness is also quite nice with curry and citrus marinades. The less dry versions can stand on their own as sipping wines very well.

And, last but certainly not the least on the list of white wines is the ever-popular Chardonnay: a dry, very full-bodied rich wine. Most wine producers age Chardonnay in oak barrels, giving it a buttery or "oaky" flavor. However, Australian winemakers do not typically age this particular wine in oak, so those from "down under" tend to be slightly fruitier with much less bitterness or tannins. Chardonnay is a perfect pair for the richness of salmon; foods dipped in butter, rich sauces like Hollandaise or cream sauces. As for cooking with Chardonnay, I prefer white wine sauces without the oak flavor, so I choose Australian Chardonnay when preparing sauce with this varietal.

And now, on to the reds. The lightest red wines are the pink wines, or rosés, like White Zinfandel. They tend to have a slight bit more body than the lightest whites, with a hint of sweetness. They are fruity, but have a slightly acidic bite, and balance well with grilled vegetables or fish, and picnic fare. Serve these wines chilled.

A very refreshing, distinctively fruity wine, meant to be drunk within a year of the vintage is Gamay. Some describe it as strawberry jam. It is nice on its own, with barbecue, or a light lunch.

Slightly higher up the scale in richness and intensity is Pinot Noir, an extremely versatile wine. A good Pinot Noir is a perfect match for a classic roast beef and with braised meats like rabbit, lamb, stew or risotto. It is also a great pair for grilled seafood. Pinot Noir is a classic choice for poaching many foods, including salmon and pears. It is the classic wine in the preparation of Beef Bourgignon.

A bit of a diversion from the varietals here will be to the Italian Chianti, Sangiovese, and the Spanish Rioja. These wines must be mentioned, as they are wonderful, balanced wines that stand up to spicy foods and game. They tend to be a bit more rustic, and not as complex or as dry and full-bodied as the Cabernets. Chianti is the lightest, with a characteristic spiciness. to me it has a festive quality. Rioja tends to be smooth and seamless. Sangiovese can be very full-bodied and complex but not quite as much as a Cabernet. The tannins are much less dramatic and aggressive. In their home countries of Italy and Spain, these wonderfully flavored red wines are drunk with most meals regardless of menu. Italian and Spanish foods favor simpler combinations spotlighting the individual flavors of each food. Sauces tend to be spicy and simple. Think pasta and sauce.

Classic red Zinfandel is a medium full-bodied wine, favoring berries, pepper and spice. It has a sort of racy streak, compatible with grilled meats and spicier foods.

Syrah or Shiraz is softer and has fewer tannins than the Cabernets, but still has the full-bodied texture and flavor, often associated with pepper. Described as a voluptuous wine, it pairs well with such full-flavored dishes as sausage, lamb, or pork with rich sauce with charm and grace.

The smoothest or most seamless of red wines is Merlot. It is slightly fruitier but has less tannin and is slightly less intense than Cabernet. Merlot tends to be a bit more sophisticated than Chianti, Sangiovese or Rioja, so will pair nicely with more sophisticated foods, and lighter but more complex sauces. This is a smooth wine; it couples well with smooth foods, like polenta or smoked tomato sauce.

Cabernet Sauvignon is a very sensual wine, full-bodied in texture and flavor, rich aroma, and a beautiful deep dark red color. Its flavor tends to be very complex, and the wine stands up to very complex dishes like spicy meats, roast leg of lamb, filet mignon. Think rich, complex flavors like steaks with pepper and Roquefort butter.

To easily learn more about a particular varietal, I suggest you choose different selections of the same varietal for the next four of five times you order or purchase wine. For example, stick to Sauvignon Blanc for the next few times you drink wine. Try those from different vintners. You will have the opportunity to taste and remember the similarities of the grape, and hopefully enjoy a great glass of wine, learning all the while. Here's to you!

Appendix

Appendix

GENERAL TEMPERATURE CHART

CHICKEN STOCK

BEEF STOCK

ROASTED VEGETABLE STOCK

BIBLIOGRAPHY

MASTER RECIPE LIST

SIDEBAR MASTER LIST

INDEX

General Temperature Chart

This chart can guide you in cooking meats to their desired doneness. There are basically three temperature zones to which most proteins are cooked.

Food:	RARE (120-140°F) (50-60°C)	MEDIUM (145-155°F) (63-68°C)	WELL-DONE (160-180°F) (76-85°C)
Poultry, Rabbit		XXXXX	
Beef, Lamb	XXXXX	XXXXX	XXXXX
Pork		XXXXX	
Veal	XLoinX		XXXXX
Kidney, Liver		XXXXX	
Fish, Shellfish	XXXXX		
Eggs	XXXXX	XXXXX	

Other important temperatures in cooking:

Simmer is 185°F, a **slow boil** is 205°F, a **rolling boil** is 212°F.

Protein begins to firm around 120°F [49°C].

Connective tissue, like gelatin, begins to soften at 120°F [49°C].

ALL proteins begin to toughen at 170°F [77°C].

Pasteurization temperature, which kills foodborne pathogens, is 140°F [60°C].

Foodborne bacteria can be destroyed by heat and rendered inactive and unable to multiply by cold. They can survive and grow in temperatures from 40-140°F [4-60°C], but will multiply most rapidly at temperatures near to those of the human body, 97-100°F [36-40°C]. At temperatures slightly above or below this zone they can still multiply, but more slowly. At 145°F [62°C] they begin to die. Below 40°F [4°C], though they are not killed, they cannot multiply quickly and are therefore harmless until allowed to get warm and lively.

Trichina pathogens can carry trichinosis in pork. These pathogens are destroyed when pork is cooked to an internal temperature of 131°F and stays at that temperature for 10 minutes, or when the pork reaches an internal temperature of 137°F. Freezing pork to below −10°F for two weeks will also kill trichina pathogens.

Chicken Stock

Good rich stock is an essential element for good sauces. A simple, rich chicken stock is a staple for great cooking, whether it is homemade or purchased.

2 – 3 pounds chicken bones, trimmed of fat
    (necks and backs work well, as do breast bones)
2 onions, peeled and quartered
2 carrots, washed and cut into 1-inch chunks
2 ribs celery, washed cut into 1-inch chunks
2 cloves garlic, peeled
1 teaspoon black peppercorns
4 sprigs fresh thyme
1 bay leaf
2 parsley stems

Combine all the ingredients in a pot that holds at least 10 quarts. Add enough COLD water to cover three-quarters of the ingredients. Bring the stock to a boil, lower the heat and simmer uncovered for four hours, skimming occasionally. Strain, pressing on solids to extract as much liquid as possible. Taste and reduce for flavor if necessary. Chill immediately in an ice bath or in the refrigerator. When chilled, skim off the fat.

Yields about 3 quarts rich stock.

COOKING CLASS

STOCK SECRETS

Great stock is flavored by your choice of meat, fowl or fish bones, aromatic vegetables and herbs. Stocks may be made with many meats, but NEVER PORK OR LAMB. Don't waste time trying to make stock from leftover bones of cooked meat; their flavor has already been leached into the cooked meat. START WITH RAW BONES. Roasting the bones and vegetables can add flavor depth and color to your finished stock. Smaller bones release flavor and gelatin more quickly than larger ones. Thus fish stock cooks in a half hour, beef stock takes 4 to 6.

START WITH COLD WATER. The slow heating of the liquid with the bones just to the boiling point helps to extract maximum protein and flavor. As soon as the stock reaches the boiling point, reduce the heat. High heat and rapid boiling make for poor quality stock.

DON'T USE TOO MUCH LIQUID. For a full-flavored stock, add only enough water to come three-quarters of the way to the top of the ingredients. The solid ingredients will settle in the cooking process.

Barely SIMMER THE STOCK. Simmering temperature is 160°F, considerably lower than boiling! You should see only an occasional bubble or two. The long slow simmer releases large amounts of protein, as well as vitamins and fats. Gelatin is extracted from the bones, giving the stock substance. Vegetables and herbs release pectin, starches, acids and more, to round out the flavor and aroma.

To prevent cloudiness, DON'T STIR THE STOCK, BUT SKIM FREQUENTLY. Cook uncovered.

When the stock is done, STRAIN off the meat and vegetables, pressing on the solids to extract as much flavor as possible. At this point you may reduce the stock by boiling it. Store it properly.

**MEAT GLAZES AND
VEGETABLE ESSENCES**

Glazes are meat or fowl stocks that have been slowly cooked down (reduced) to a thick syrup. These are handy to have on hand because they require much less storage space and can be reconstituted into stock simply by adding water. Glaze can be added to a sauce at the last minute to give a richer flavor, deeper color, and a smoother texture.

Essences are extracts made from vegetable stock and used as last minute flavorings for sauces.

If you have limited freezer space or just want to have some glaze around for quick sauces, boil any stock down until it becomes sticky and coats the back of a spoon. One quart of stock will yield 4 ounces of meat glaze. Boil rapidly at the beginning, but lower the heat toward the end to prevent burning.

Meat glazes and vegetable essences are used to reinforce sauces or as a base for butter sauces. They can easily be reconstituted ($1/2$ cup glaze or essence to $3 1/2$ cups water) to make stock again. They freeze easily.

Beef Stock

Rich beef stock makes great meat glaze, a wonderful flavoring agent for your recipes. Check out the directions on the sidebar. Give it a try!

3 – 4 pounds meaty beef or veal bones, or a combination
2 onions, quartered
2 carrots, cut into 1-inch chunks
2 ribs celery, cut into 1-inch chunks
2 cloves garlic, peeled
1 teaspoon black peppercorns
4 sprigs fresh thyme
1 bay leaf
2 parsley stems

Heat the oven to 450°F. Spread the bones in large shallow roasting pans and roast for 40 minutes or until well browned. Turn the bones, add the onions, carrots and celery, and roast 20 minutes more. Transfer the roasted bones and vegetables to a pot that holds at least 10 quarts. Discard the fat from the roasting pans. Place the roasting pans on the stove over medium heat. Add 2 cups of water to the roasting pans to "deglaze" the pans, scraping up the browned bits as you bring it to a boil. Add the "deglazing" liquid to the stockpot, along with the garlic, peppercorns and herbs. Add enough COLD water to cover three-quarters of the ingredients.

Bring the stockpot to a boil over high heat. Immediately lower the heat and simmer the stock, uncovered, for 5 to 6 hours, skimming occasionally. Pour the stock through a strainer, pressing on the solids to extract as much liquid as possible. Taste and reduce for flavor if necessary. Chill immediately in an ice bath or in the refrigerator. When chilled, skim off the fat. *(See the sidebar on p. 173 about storing stocks safely.)*

Yields about 3 quarts rich stock or 12 ounces meat glaze.

Roasted Vegetable Stock

2 – 4 tablespoons olive oil
2 large leeks, halved and washed, white and light green parts only
1 onion, quartered
3 carrots, cut into 1-inch chunks
3 ribs celery, cut into 1-inch chunks
2 parsnips, cut into 1-inch chunks
1 turnip, cut into 1-inch chunks
1 fennel bulb quartered
3 large tomatoes, halved
1 cup dry white wine
4 cloves garlic, peeled
1 teaspoon black peppercorns
4 sprigs fresh thyme
1 bay leaf
2 parsley stems

Heat the oven to 450°F. Grease a large shallow roasting pan with the olive oil. Spread the vegetables in the prepared pan and roast for 20 to 40 minutes or until well browned, turning occasionally. Transfer the roasted vegetables to a stockpot that holds at least 12 quarts. Discard the fat from the roasting pan. Place the roasting pan on the stove over medium heat. Add the wine to "deglaze" the roasting pan, scraping up the browned bits as you bring it to a boil. Add the "deglazing" liquid to the stockpot, along with the garlic, peppercorns and herbs. Add enough COLD water to cover three-quarters of the ingredients.

Bring the stockpot to a boil over high heat. Immediately lower the heat and simmer the stock, uncovered, for 2½ to 3 hours, skimming occasionally. Pour the stock through a strainer, pressing on the solids to extract as much liquid as possible. Taste and reduce for flavor if necessary. Chill immediately in an ice bath or in the refrigerator. When chilled, skim off any fat.

Yields about 2 quarts rich stock.

COOKING CLASS

STORING STOCKS SAFELY

Homemade stock is easily prepared in bulk and frozen in smaller portions for later use. Your finished stock can be reduced to one-fourth volume to reduce the required storage space. Boil the strained stock rapidly at the beginning, then gradually lower the heat to prevent burning in the end.

Reducing a stock and freezing it in Mason jars (clearly indicating dates) works well. Smaller quantities of chilled stock can be poured into resealable plastic bags and frozen flat for quick defrosting. Or freeze the stock in an ice tray, then transfer the cubes to a resealable plastic bag. Frozen stocks store without a signifi cant loss of flavor up to 6 months. Refrigerate stock no more than three days. **Always reboil stock after chilling or freezing to ensure all pathogens have been destroyed**.

Cool stocks quickly. Warm stock is a perfect medium for bacteria. Avoid keeping stocks at temperatures most favored by bacteria, between 40°F and 140°F, for long periods. Since a quart of stock is a relatively small amount which will cool quickly, it can be allowed to cool for a short period of time at room temperature before refrigeration or freezing, with little danger of spoilage. Larger amounts are best cooled by dividing them into smaller quantities, or by floating a container of ice in the stock to chill it before putting it into the refrigerator. Large amounts of stock may require several batches of ice.

Bibliography

Conway, Linda Glick, ed. *The Culinary Institute of America, The New Professional Chef, Fifth Edition.* New York, New York: Van Nostrand Reinhold, 1991.

Cook's Illustrated editors. *The Best Recipe.* Brookline, Massachusetts: Boston Common Press, 1999.

Corriher, Shirley O. *CookWise.* New York, New York: William Morrow and Company, Inc.: 1997.

Elving, Phyllis, ed. *Sunset Fresh Produce.* Menlo Park, California: Lane Publishing Company, 1987.

Goldstein, Sid. *The Wine Lover's Cookbook.* San Francisco, California: Chronicle Books, 1999.

Herbst, Sharon Tyler. *Food Lover's Companion.* Hauppage, New York: Barron's Educational Series, Inc., 1990.

Hillman, Howard. *Kitchen Science, Revised Edition.* Boston, Massachusetts: Houghton Mifflin Company, 1981.

Ingram, Christine. *The Cook's Guide to Vegetables.* London, England: Anness Publishing, Ltd., 1999.

Kowalchik, Claire & Hylton, William H., ed. *Rodale's Illustrated Encyclopedia of Herbs.* Emmaus, Pennsylvania: Rodale Press, 1987.

Peterson, James. *Sauces: Classical and Contemporary Sauce Making.* New York, New York: Van Nostrand Reinhold, 1991.

Piccolo, Jack. *Timing is Everything.* New York, New York: Three Rivers Press, 2000.

St. Pierre, Brian. *A Perfect Glass of Wine.* San Francisco, California: Chronicle Books, 1996.

Master Recipe List

Sidebar Master List

Sidebar Master List

Index

Index

Index

ORDER FORM

Name _____

Address _____

City _____ State _____ Zip _____

Phone (_____) _____

       Please send me _____ books @ $24.95/book $ _____

       S & H: $5.00 for first book $ _____

       S & H: $3.00 for each additional book $ _____

       Washington State Residents add 8.8% Sales Tax $ _____

       Total enclosed $ _____

Mail to:
Carol Dearth
Fork in the Road Publishers
1883 145th Place Southeast
Bellevue, Washington 98007

For additional information:
(425) 644-4285
raincitycookingschool.com